The Disciple Maker

THE DISCIPLE MAKER

Published with permission by Onnuri English Ministry

THE
DISCIPLE
MAKER

지은이 | A discipleship resource of Onnuri English Ministry
초판 발행 | 2014. 4. 14.
등록번호 | 제3-203호
등록된 곳 | 서울특별시 용산구 서빙고로65길 38
발행처 | 사단법인 두란노서원
영업부 | 2078-3333 FAX | 080-749-3705
출판부 | 2078-3477

▮ 책 값은 뒤표지에 있습니다.
ISBN 978-89-531-2036-5 03230

▮ 독자의 의견을 기다립니다.
tpress@duranno.com www.duranno.com

두란노서원은 바울 사도가 3차 전도여행 때 에베소에서 성령 받은 제자들을 따로 세워 하나님의 말씀으로 양육하던 장소입니다. 사도행전 19장 8–20절의 정신에 따라 첫째 목회자를 돕는 사역과 평신도를 훈련시키는 사역, 둘째 세계선교TIM 와 문서선교 단행본 · 잡지 사역, 셋째 예수문화 및 경배와 찬양 사역, 그리고 가정 · 상담 사역 등을 감당하고 있습니다. 1980년 12월 22일에 창립된 두란노서원은 주님 오실 때까지 이 사역들을 계속할 것입니다.

THE **DISCIPLE** MAKER

A discipleship resource of Onnuri English Ministry

Duranno

EDITORS

Eddie Byun

Joel Yoon

CONTRIBUTORS

Joel Yoon

Eddie Byun

Kent Lee

Daniel Park

Special thanks to Pastor Yong Jo Ha and Pastor Jae Hoon Lee for their visionary leadership. Thanks also to Mike Lee, Rebekah McNay, Heather Hong, Jacob Bennett, Jonathan English, Angela Sommers, Daniel Sanchez and Joanne Kim for your thoughts, suggestions and help.

Thank you to the OEM community that strives to finish the mission by raising disciples of Christ one person at a time!

ABOUT THE EDITORS

Eddie Byun (D.Min., Gordon-Conwell Theological Seminary) is lead pastor at Onnuri English Ministry (OEM), the English-speaking ministry of Onnuri Community Church in Seoul, Korea. He is also the author of *Justice Awakening*.

Joel Yoon (M.Div., Covenant Theological Seminary) serves as the discipleship pastor at Onnuri English Ministry (OEM) in Seoul, Korea. He leads the One-to-One Discipleship Ministry at OEM. His passion is to see each believer engaging in the Great Commission by equipping disciples to make disciples.

CONTRIBUTORS

Kent Lee, Ph.D., University of Illinois @ Urbana-Champaign

Daniel Park, M.Div., Torch Trinity Theological Seminary

TABLE OF CONTENTS

INTRODUCTION

"Discipling is an intentional relationship in which we walk alongside other disciples in order to encourage, equip and challenge one another in love to grow toward maturity in Christ. This includes equipping the disciple to teach others as well." -Greg Ogden

One of the greatest misunderstandings within Christianity is the illusion that the goal of a Christian in outreach is to make converts. Nowhere in the Bible does it say that we are to seek conversion as the end goal. If we do, we have sadly misunderstood the mission and really, the heart of Jesus.

Jesus, in the Great Commission, says, "All authority in heaven and on earth has been given to me. Therefore go and make disciples of all nations, baptizing them in the name of the Father and of the Son and of the Holy Spirit, and teaching them to obey everything I have commanded you. And surely I am with you always, to the very end of the age" (Matthew 28:18-20). What does this teach us about what it means to be a disciple?

First, we see that disciples are baptized. Baptism is a physical sign of a spiritual reality - that a person has come to be converted to faith in Jesus Christ. Second, we see that disciples are to obey everything Jesus has commanded. Notice that Jesus does not say to simply know everything that God has taught, but to obey everything that God has taught. Conversion is just the beginning of the discipleship journey! Conversion is coming to know Christ. Obedience is learning to obey Christ, whom you have come to know. The reason we obey, the reason we do discipleship, is because we have now entered into a real relationship with Christ.

The goal of this book is not behavior modification. The goal of this book is coming to know Christ deeply and learning his teachings, which will then lead to life change. Obedience stems from a person, not a set of rules. Let us come to know the person of Jesus Christ more deeply through this book!

How do we do this at Onnuri English Ministry (OEM)? That is where One-to-One Discipleship comes in, the purpose of which is as follows: "Raising and releasing Kingdom workers by meeting, mentoring and multiplying another disciple."

One-to-One is a 9-part discipleship resource that you will do with a mentor. We recognize that discipleship does not happen in a program, but in doing life together. The heart of the One-to-One ministry is that through this program, you would truly learn to do life together, and the lessons that are learned won't only be through the content of this material, but through walking together with your mentor. During your time together, you will look at the following topics: the Bible, God, the biblical story, repentance, worship, community, discipleship, service, and outreach. But in addition, ask your mentor questions. Study the Bible together. Serve the church or do an outreach together. Learn from your mentor by doing life together.

HOW DO I USE THIS BOOK?

Each section includes Interaction, Introduction, Instruction, Take Away, and Intercession.

Interaction is for you to begin dialoging with the subject. It asks basic questions to help your mind prepare for the lesson. Do not skip this section. It is only when we know what we don't know that we are ready to learn. Answer these questions to the best of your ability. In doing so, your mind and heart will be in a better posture to learn.

Introduction will establish the importance of that topic in your mind and heart.

Instruction is where the lesson is taught. These are the longest and most difficult sections. We have found that most books of this nature do not ask difficult and challenging questions. By doing so, books of this nature have become boring and even tedious to go through. We have decided to put a book out there that trusts that the reader truly wants to grow and is willing to be challenged and pushed so that the disciple can become more like Christ. Don't go through this book half-heartedly, but take the challenge and give God all of your heart, mind, and strength because God is going to be pouring Himself into you through these sessions. Don't miss out on these blessings!

We believe that all the lessons and principles that are necessary for the growth of a disciple of Christ are revealed in Scripture. This section includes not only content that needs to be learned, but also steps towards real application of that truth in your life. Answer both content and application questions before meeting with your mentor so that you can get the most out of your discussions.

Take Away gives you an opportunity to review the lesson and apply the topic at hand. For this section, think about the following: head, heart, or hands. Write down specifically the following: 1) What you learned and what you would like to remember; 2) How this topic impacts your heart - what did you learn about who you are in Christ? 3) How will this affect how you live? With that, try to be specific and concrete. It should be measurable meaning, the following week, your mentor should be able to ask you how you applied the lesson in your life and you should be able to respond with a practical example from your week. An application like, "I will love people more this week" is not a measurable application. An application like, "I will do lunch with my co-worker" or "I will read the Bible in the mornings before work" is measurable.

Intercession has a two-fold purpose. Prayer is a huge means of grace given to the disciple, but yet is such an underdeveloped practice in the life of the average Christian. Through this ministry, you will learn the truths about prayer, but through this section, you will learn to put those truths of prayer into practice. In addition, Christ wants all his disciples to continue to mature. We will play our part by praying through these topics for yourself, the church, the city and the nations. Pray on your own as you prepare for each session, and also pray out-loud with your mentor for these topics.

For more information, please email: discipleship@onnurienglish.org.
All Scripture is from the English Standard Version (ESV).

BIBLE: GOD'S SELF-REVELATION

In the beginning was the Word, and the Word was with God, and the Word was God. -John 1:1

The Bible is alive, it speaks to me; it has feet, it runs after me; it has hands, it lays hold of me.

-Martin Luther

INTERACTION

What is your understanding of the Bible? How would you describe it to a non-believer?

___

___

___

What role does it have in your life right now? Why?

___

___

How often do you read the Bible?

- Everyday
- 2-3 times a week
- Once a week
- Once a month
- Rarely/Never

When you read the Bible, how long do you read it?

- 1+ hour/s
- 30+ minutes
- 15+ minutes
- 10+ minutes
- Couple minutes

When you read the Bible, do you find it challenging to receive something from it?

___

___

What are some reasons you don't read the Bible more?

___

___

INTRODUCTION

WHAT IS THE BIBLE?

God is God and we are not. God is creator and we are creation. God is entirely other. This is why, apart from Jesus and the Holy Spirit, the Bible is the greatest gift God has given to His people. It is His self-revelation.

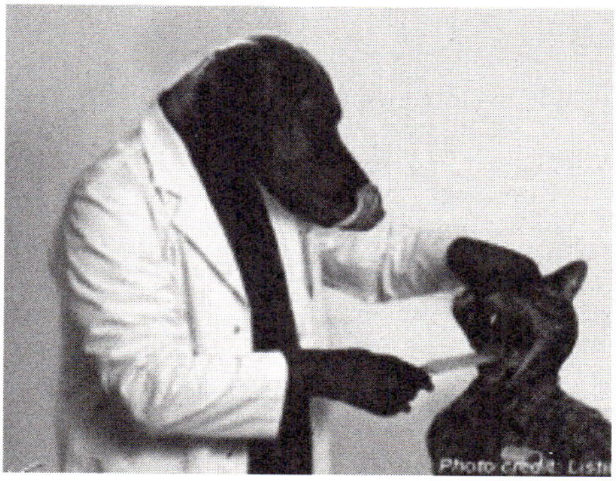

I saw a picture the other day of a dog dressed up as a dentist checking the teeth of a cat. Ridiculous! It's comical because we know that though a dog is able to think at a certain capacity, he is unable to function as a dentist, much less to a feline! So knowing that a finite dog cannot comprehend the complexities of the mind of a finite man, how much more difficult is it for a finite man to understand an infinite God?

This is how much God loves man. He desires for us to know Him so much that He gave us a way that our finite minds can comprehend

Him. If God did not reveal Himself to us, it would be impossible to know Him. The Word of God is the lens to be able to see God and to know God.

HOW DO WE HAVE THE BIBLE IN ITS FORM TODAY?

God loves to do the extraordinary through the ordinary. We see this throughout scripture and history. God chose to come to man in the form of an ordinary man to do the extraordinary work of saving the world to Himself. God entrusted twelve ordinary men of ordinary skill to do the extraordinary work of starting the church and spreading the gospel to the ends of the earth. And in the same way, God chose ordinary men through the ordinary means of writing, to do the extraordinary work of revealing Himself to us.

The Bible is the self-revelation of God. By reading it and knowing it, we come to know God. As opposed to using super-natural means, He gave us the Bible through the ordinary means of ordinary people through ordinary writing. So God raised up many men to write the sixty-six books of the Bible over 1,600 years. When you read the Bible from Genesis to Revelation, you will realize that it is remarkably uniform and consistent. This is something that you will realize more and more as you study and understand scripture. You will start to see that though there were over 40 different authors of the books of the Bible, God was the main author through it all. He inspired it all. As you read the Bible you will see that all the stories of scripture form a mosaic of one grand narrative.

This is all the more evident when you think about how the message of the Bible has been preserved so well. There exists 3,000 Hebrew manuscripts of the Old Testament and 5,700 Greek manuscripts of the New Testament. The next most copied piece of literature of the first and second century only has 75 copies!

The translators of the ESV write that the "significant variants affect far less than 1 percent of the words of the ESV text, and even among that 1 percent, there are no variants that would change any point of doctrine."

Although this does not prove the Bible's claim, it reveals to us that the Bible is not like other books. God's hand was upon it and as He inspired men to write, He also kept its message pure. Through the ordinary means of men, through the extraordinary power of the Holy Spirit, we have the inspired and inerrant Word of God. *God has spoken and He has spoken through the Bible!*

INSTRUCTION

As we learn more about Scripture, let's see what the Bible says about itself.

- 2 Timothy 3:16-17 ____

  ____

- John 1:1 ____

  ____

As we come to read and know the Word of God, we actually come to know God Himself. God did not simply save us from hell, but He made a way for us to be with Him in heaven. Furthermore, we learn that God saved us so that we may begin our personal and intimate relationship with Him here on earth. He desires for us to truly and deeply know Him. To cultivate this personal relationship, we want to learn to intentionally seek Him.

In order to do this, many people keep a Quiet Time. A Quiet Time is simply that, a quiet time, unhindered by the common distractions of the world, set apart from our busy day, so that we can have a focused intimate time with Him. As we are now in relationship with Him, we want to cultivate our personal relationship and intimate walk with the Lord through prayer and Scripture. It's a time to be still and learn from God, listen to God, and live in light of His presence.

WHAT DOES THE BIBLE HAVE TO SAY ABOUT THE IMPORTANCE OF HAVING QUIET TIMES?

Charles Spurgeon was once asked, "How do you defend the Bible?" "Very easy", he responded. "The same way I defend a lion. I simply let it out of its cage." The Bible has power because it is God's Word. And God is powerful.

As you read these verses below, what does each verse reveal about Scripture and its place in our lives?

- Deuteronomy 8:3 ______________________________

____

- Psalm 25:4-5 ______________________________

____

- Psalm 119:9-11 ______________________________

____

- Psalm 119:103 ______________________________

____

- Psalm 119:105 ______________________________

____

- Romans 10:17 ______________________________

____

- Romans 12:2 ______________________________

____

- Hebrews 4:12 ______________________________

____

WHY SHOULD WE HAVE A DAILY QUIET TIME?

TO ENJOY FELLOWSHIP WITH THE LORD:

- 1 Corinthians 1:9 ______________________________

____

TO GAIN SPIRITUAL FEEDING FOR OUR SOUL:

- Matthew 4:4____

- Psalm 119:103____

TO RECEIVE DIRECTION FROM THE LORD:

- Psalm 25:4-5 ____

- Psalm 119:105____

OUT OF DEPENDENCE UPON THE LORD:

- Luke 5:15-16 ____

- Mark 1:35____

How is walking with God a sign of dependence upon Him? What message are we conveying to Him if we never meet with Him in the private place of prayer?

PRACTICAL SUGGESTIONS IN READING THE WORD

- Have a specific time (Daniel 6:10) - Daniel committed certain times of his day to spend focused time on the Lord. Give God your best time, not your left over time.
- Have a special place.(Luke 22:39; Mark 1:35) - Jesus had His "usual" place that became His place of fellowship with His Father in heaven. Soon that special place will be a sacred place where you know you will meet the Lord and hear from Him. For many people, it is very helpful to have a set place.
- Have a simple plan. Don't focus on rules, focus on your relationship with Christ. Enjoy Him. Enjoy His presence and get to know Him through His Word.

  Do you have a devoted time and place for each day? Make a plan to devote a time and place to seek God today, tomorrow and each day this week that can be repeated weekly.

Sunday	
Monday	
Tuesday	
Wednesday	
Thursday	
Friday	
Saturday	

HERE IS A SIMPLE PLAN OF ACTION YOU CAN TRY:

- **Relax - Matthew 11:28**

  We live in a busy world and often feel like we're in a rush. But this is a time to be still before the Lord and learn to rest in His presence.

- **Rejoice - Psalm 150**

  Praise Him for His goodness and love. Let your focus be upon the greatness of our God!

- **Request - Psalm 119:18; Psalm 139:23-24**

  Ask the Lord to open your eyes so that you can see the wonderful things in His Word. Ask God to speak to your heart.

- **Reflect - Psalm 119:15, 97**

  Read, reflect, and meditate on God's Words.

- **Record - Deuteronomy 6:8-9**

  Write down things that impact you during your time of reflection. If something is sticking out to you, that's God's way of saying: "Pay attention!"

- **Request - Ephesians 6:18**

  We request again during this time to intercede for other people and other needs. Pray that your life would be conformed more to the image of Jesus Christ.

- **Respond - James 1:22**

  Write down a specific action plan you'd like to live out in light of the Bible passage you read. We don't just want to listen to the Word, we want to live it out, because only application of information will bring life transformation.

DIFFERENT WAYS TO READ THE BIBLE

READ DEEP

This is the most traditional way of reading the Bible and how most people are taught to do their quiet times. They read one section of the Bible, usually a story or a chunk of thought, meditate on it, break it down and really try to understand and apply the truths of that section. This is a great way of going deeper into the Word.

READ WIDE

This is probably the second most popular way of reading the Bible. The purpose of this is to see the big picture of the Bible. The Bible is one grand narrative of God's plan of redemption for the world. It's important to study the individual stories of the Bible, but understanding the big picture of the Bible will help you properly understand the individual stories of the Bible. I challenge you to read the Bible in a short span of time. It has been said that it takes 72 hours to read the Bible from front to back. Take the challenge and read the Bible in a short span of time such as 1 year or even 3-6 months.

READ PURPOSEFULLY

I have found the number one reason people stop reading the Bible is because they grow bored of the Bible. It's like a man always practicing a sport, but never playing in a game. Without a purpose, people grow bored and passive. It is no different with the Bible. When the reader has a purpose for reading and studying the Bible, the Bible comes alive. Too often, people open up the Bible and read passively. I encourage you to be active with the Bible. Here are a few ways to make your time purposeful.

1) Dialogue with the author. Ask the Bible questions. Ask why the author would have written that verse? What was the author really trying to say?
2) Find out what the Bible says about a subject. What does the Bible actually say about salvation? If someone was to ask you, "Where in the Bible does it say that Jesus is God?" are you able to defend that? What does the Bible say about

relationships? How about making decisions in life? What will heaven be like?

3) Master a book. One thing I try to do, especially with smaller books of the Bible, is to read it over and over. I try to find the big chunks of thought of the author and really try to comprehend the whole message of the book. For example, for books like 1 John, I have read it everyday for a month, really trying to understand the purpose of 1 John. In addition, I try to outline the book and the author's train of thought. In doing so, as I become more aggressive in my reading of the Bible, I have received so much more from Scripture.

READ OVER

The authors of the books of the Bible often speak about deep and long meditation on Scripture. The Psalms often speak about how it is the Word of God that keeps them close to God and keeps them on the path of purity and righteousness. This is the picture of the true believer – one who deeply meditates on scripture. One way to do this is to memorize the Word of God. You can memorize a verse from your quiet times so that you can keep that truth with you. There are memory verse packs sold or that can be found online. These are often key scripture verses packed with truth. You can also challenge yourself to memorize larger portions of scripture, such as paragraphs, chapters and even books. May you be a man or woman meditating on the law of the Lord day and night!

We will study more about the purpose of Scripture in our lives in the worship section.

TAKE AWAYS: HEAD – HEART– HANDS

As you finish this chapter on the Bible, reflect on a few things. What are some things from this chapter that are new to you? How do those things change the way you feel towards God? How do those things change the way you view yourself? In light of these things what will you do in the coming weeks? What role do you desire for the Word of God to play in your life?

See Appendix for additional Bible resources.

Intercession

FOR YOURSELF

Pray through Psalm 119:9-16.

Pray that God might give you a greater appreciation and hunger for His Word. Ask God to give you strength, discipline, and wisdom to know how to study His Word and apply it.

FOR THE CHURCH

Pray for your pastor to faithfully preach the Word of God.

Pray that your church would be a Bible-believing, Bible-honoring, Bible-preaching, and Bible-practicing community.

FOR THE CITY

Pray for your city, that the Bible would influence how people view God and view life.

FOR THE NATIONS

The Bible is still in the process of being translated into every language. As we have learned that the Bible is the self-revelation of

God, it is foundational for a people-group to have the Bible translated in their language for that group to come to know Him. Pray for the expansion of the Bible into every country. Pray for Wycliffe, an integral ministry for the translation of the Bible.
http://www.wycliffe.org/

MEMORY VERSE

All Scripture is breathed out by God and profitable for teaching, for reproof, for correction, and for training in righteousness, that the man of God may be complete, equipped for every good work.
-2 Timothy 3:16-17

GOD: THE HOLY ONE

Worthy are you, our Lord and God, to receive glory and honor and power, for you created all things, and by your will they existed and were created. -Revelation 4:11.

Men are never duly touched and impressed with a conviction of their insignificance until they have contrasted themselves with the majesty of God.
-John Calvin

INTERACTION

In your own words, who is God to you? ______________________________

____

How would you explain who Jesus is? ______________________________

____

How about the Holy Spirit? ______________________________________

____

INTRODUCTION

In recent years the church has developed its own catch phrases for God to make Him more relevant to the fast paced culture. In the 90's "awesome" became the default-adjective for God due to the popular worship song "Our God is an Awesome God." As the years progressed "Jesus is my homeboy" became a slogan sported by Hollywood stars and 8th graders alike. Many people who have grown up in the church will remember things like "God is the best surprise ever" and "God is bigger than the boogie man" that our church curriculums, and family-friendly media used to help us understand who it is that we pray to.

While some of these phrases are fun, reminiscent, and ridiculous and may even convey some truth, the ways in which these describe God, and the thoughts we have towards Him are not to be taken lightly. We cannot really wrap our minds around God or understand Him with our limited, finite human minds. We as humans cannot even understand the mystery of the Trinity-the fact that God is three persons but one God. There is no way we can articulate His greatness within the confines of human language- much less the casual phrases that get tossed around in Christian circles.

In a culture and an age where things are ready-made and information can be boiled down to a 10-minute explanation on YouTube or the right wording in your search engine, we tend to think that we can understand God by showing up to church and talking about Him at small group. However, as we endeavor to get to know the King of the Universe, who is also our Father, we need to realize that this is a process that will take every day of the rest of our lives. Even in heaven, as the great hymn "Amazing Grace" says, after we've been there 10,000 years, "we'll have no less days to sing God's praise" because we will continually learn more of His character.

This God who is beyond our understanding has revealed Himself to us, sought us out, and forged an eternal relationship with us. He is awesome in His power and in His deep love.
Our focus is on understanding how God has revealed Himself to us in Scripture – what He wants us to understand about who He is. Scripture describes God's character or nature – what He is like and what He does. So in this chapter we will explore God's attributes – His characteristics – and the functions or roles of the Father, Son, and Spirit. Finally, we'll talk about what this all means for us practically.

INSTRUCTION

In the time of Jesus and the early Church, there were some unusual views of God that were popular, as well as misconceptions of who the God of the Bible really was. There were also many false gods from competing religions. Jesus entered into this confusion to bring us clarity, and to tell us who God really is, and what He wants. Today there are also some unusual views of God in popular culture. Today we also encounter competition from many false gods – the idols of materialism, selfishness, pleasure, and many other idols. Into this chaos Jesus comes to declare today that He is God, and that He came to save us and to bring us into a relationship with the true God of the universe. This Jesus is the same as God the Father, in character and nature (Hebrews 1:1-4). In the Old Testament, we see God, simply referred to as God, and other very reverential names like Almighty and Lord. Then along comes Jesus, who asked us to follow Him – to surrender our lives and everything, and to be His disciples. Jesus talked about Himself in divine terms, and He talked about God the Father. In fact, Jesus didn't only refer to Him as "Lord," but He also addressed Him as "Father," which was a surprisingly intimate way to address God back then. Jesus then introduces the Holy Spirit.

The Holy Spirit is hinted at in the Old Testament, but He becomes more prominent as Jesus starts His public ministry. In Mark 1:9-11 we see Jesus being baptized, and the Father speaking from heaven as the Holy Spirit comes upon Jesus. It is from passages like this where two or more members of the Trinity interact that we realize that God is complex. Scripture declares that He is one ("Hear, O Israel: The Lord our God, the Lord is one" - Deuteronomy 6:4) and is the only God who exists or ever existed. Yet we see Him simultaneously in three persons, as Father, Son and Spirit.

Although the Trinity is very complex, Scripture speaks of the Trinity very simply. We see this most often when the Bible speaks of the Trinity working together. We also see Jesus was involved in the creation (John 1:1-3; Col 1:16-17), and Genesis 1 hints of the Spirit's involvement. In Ephesians 1, we see the full cooperation of the Trinity in the redemption plan.

As believers, we interact with each of them and all of them together, and we often address this triune Father-Son-Spirit simply as "God." Jesus reconciles us to God, and as God who became a man, He reveals God to us. He helps us to see and understand God. The Spirit draws us to Jesus, and gives us rebirth. The Spirit fills us, empowers us, and makes God's presence known to us. This awesome triune God is always at work in our lives. Though God is beyond our mind's comprehension, we can have a deep, personal relationship with Him.

We will continue to learn more about the ministry of the Father, Son and the Holy Spirit throughout this book. So let's take a deeper look at understanding God the Father, God the Son, and God the Holy Spirit.

GOD THE FATHER

In Matthew 6:8, Jesus teaches His disciples to address God as "Our Father" when we pray. This was shocking for the disciples. They thought of God as holy and so to think of a holy God as your "heavenly father" was humbling. Read Matthew 6:5-13. What do you think these disciples were thinking when they heard this?

____

____

____

Our relationship with our earthly father often carries over to our relationship with our heavenly father. Consider Romans 8:15-17, where Paul uses "abba," an intimate term in the ancient Aramaic language that is like "daddy." What does that tell us about how we should view God?

____

____

____

Take a moment and pray to Him now with the mindset that you are His beloved child. Use language like "dad" or "daddy" to help you embrace the attitude of a child. Was there anything that was different?

____

____

____

GOD THE SON: JESUS CHRIST

Jesus is as popular as ever. He has been discussed, depicted, and debated from the most liberal to the most conservative in media. Jesus is the most controversial figure in history. From the time He lived on Earth to the very moment you are reading this, He has been debated. The primary difference between Judaism and Christianity is

Jesus. Islam believes Jesus was a prophet, but not God. Some people love Him and some people hate Him. And rightly so. Because Jesus was so radical in His actions and His teachings, people either wanted Him dead or were willing to die for Him. Let's take a look at what Jesus said about Himself. What did Jesus claim in these passages?

- Luke 5:20-21 ____

____

- John 3:16-18 ____

____

- John 8:46-47 ____

____

- John 10:25-30 ____

____

In Mere Christianity, C.S. Lewis writes about the way in which Jesus viewed Himself.

> *I am trying here to prevent anyone saying the really foolish thing that people often say about Him: 'I'm ready to accept Jesus as a great moral teacher, but I don't accept His claim to be God.' That is the one thing we must not say. A man who was merely a man and said the sort of things Jesus said would not be a great moral teacher. He would either*

be a lunatic— on a level with the man who says he is a poached egg— or else he would be the Devil of Hell. You must make your choice. Either this man was, and is, the Son of God: or else a madman or something worse. You can shut Him up for a fool, you can spit at Him and kill Him as a demon; or you can fall at His feet and call Him Lord and God. But let us not come with any patronising nonsense about His being a great human teacher. He has not left that open to us. He did not intend to. [1]

Lewis so succinctly writes that Jesus was either a Lord, lunatic or a liar. Because we believe that Jesus is Lord, we trust Him with every part of our lives.

What does the Bible say about Jesus being the Lord of our lives?

- Matthew 7:21-23 ____

____

- Luke 6:46-49 ____

____

Are there areas in your life that you have not fully surrendered to Him?

1 C. S. Lewis, (2009-05-28). *Mere Christianity* (C.S. Lewis Signature Classics) (p. 52). HarperCollins. Kindle Edition.

HOLY SPIRIT

From the Godhead, the Holy Spirit is often the most misunderstood and certainly the most controversial within Christian circles. It is very important that we know the ministry of the Holy Spirit so that we can fully receive the work of the Holy Spirit.

There are a few references to the Holy Spirit in the Old Testament (Psalm 51:11; Isaiah 63:10, 11). However, this changes in the New Testament. The Holy Spirit is explicitly mentioned over 260 times. It is littered all over the gospels, but we have the clearest teaching about the role and purpose of the Holy Spirit from Jesus when He introduces the Holy Spirit.

In Acts 1:4-8, what are the disciples commanded to do? And why? What do we learn about the Holy Spirit from this passage?

____

____

____

The Bible mentions various roles of the Holy Spirit in our lives. What has the Holy Spirit done in your life? Below is a list of some of the things that the Spirit does for us. Pick three of these, and meditate on them for a while; ask the Spirit to show Himself to you, and to show you how He has been working in you. Then be ready to share how the Spirit has been working in these three areas of your life.

- Spiritual rebirth [2 Cor. 1:22; John 3:6; John 6:63]
- Assurance of salvation [Rom. 8:16, 1 John 4:13, 1 John 3:24]
- Sanctifying us [2 Thess. 2:13, 1 Peter 1:2]
- Means of spiritual living [Gal. 5:16]
- Fellowship with God [1 John 3:24]
- Access to God [Eph. 2:18]
- Empowering us [Judges 6:34 (Gideon); Acts 4:31]
- Helping us to pray [Rom. 8:26]; means of prayer [Jude 1:20]

- Convicting people of sin [John 16:8-11]
- Teaching and guiding us [John 14:26, 16:12-15]
- Filling us [Acts 2, Acts 13:52, Eph. 5:17-19]

____

____

____

____

____

____

The Spirit is described as our "Comforter" or "Helper" (see John 14:26). The sense of the word in the original Greek (in which the New Testament was first written) is like one who comes alongside you. What does it mean that God's Spirit is actually with you, always by your side?

SPIRIT-FILLED LIFE

Col. 2:6 Therefore, as you received Christ Jesus the Lord, so walk in him, 7 rooted and built up in him and established in the faith, just as you were taught, abounding in thanksgiving.

Just as you purposefully chose to receive Christ, we are called to purposefully walk with Him. This is also known as walking by the Spirit. When you put your faith and trust in Christ, the Holy Spirit came into your heart to reside in you. But as scripture so often states, though we are given the Holy Spirit, we are still called to choose to "walk by the Spirit." Read Galatians 5:16-24 and circle and highlight what it means to "walk by the Spirit."

> *Gal. 5:16 But I say, walk by the Spirit, and you will not gratify the desires of the flesh. 17 For the desires of the flesh are against the Spirit, and the desires of the Spirit are against the flesh, for these are opposed to each other, to keep you from doing the things you want to do. 18 But if you are led by the Spirit, you are not under the law. 19 Now the works of the flesh are evident: sexual immorality, impurity, sensuality, 20 idolatry, sorcery, enmity, strife, jealousy, fits of anger, rivalries, dissensions, divisions, 21 envy, drunkenness, orgies, and things like these. I warn you, as I warned you before, that those who do such things will not inherit the kingdom of God. 22 But the fruit of the Spirit is love, joy, peace, patience, kindness, goodness, faithfulness, 23 gentleness, self-control; against such things there is no law. 24 And those who belong to Christ Jesus have crucified the flesh with its passions and desires.*

What did you learn about walking by the Spirit and the battle against sin?

____

____

____

____

Notice that when you walk by the Spirit, you bear "fruit," not "fruits." It is all a by-product of the Spirit of God making known His love in your heart. In order to gauge our spiritual walk, let's take a look at the fruit of the Spirit in our lives.

	Low				*High*
Love	*1*	*2*	*3*	*4*	*5*
Joy	*1*	*2*	*3*	*4*	*5*
Peace	*1*	*2*	*3*	*4*	*5*
Patience	*1*	*2*	*3*	*4*	*5*
Kindness	*1*	*2*	*3*	*4*	*5*
Goodness	*1*	*2*	*3*	*4*	*5*
Gentleness	*1*	*2*	*3*	*4*	*5*
Self-Control	*1*	*2*	*3*	*4*	*5*

Are you as filled with the Spirit as you would like to be? If not, what are the reasons you lack the fruit of the Spirit?

____

____

____

Scripture has many references to what it means to walk by the Spirit. Similar to walking by the Spirit is what Scripture refers to as "abiding in God." Read the following passages and write down different elements of how to walk by the Spirit or to abide in God.

Match the passages below to the appropriate application.

John 15:9	Praise
Ephesians 5:17-19	Repentance
1John 1:7	Obedience
1John 1:8-10	Word
1 John 2:24	Fellowship

These are critical components of living by the Spirit. These are the means of grace in which God desires to fill us with his Spirit. Reflect on these words and ask God which of these areas you need to grow in?

- Word
- Repentance
- Obedience
- Fellowship
- Praise

GOD'S ATTRIBUTES

Discuss what each of these attributes means to you personally. How do you feel when you think and meditate about each of these?

- Eternal, or self-existent: God simply exists by Himself. No one created Him, He simply existed. And it was from God that time, life, creation, people, and everything else is created. There is no one greater than God. He was there before the beginning (Gen 1:1, Psalm 90:2).
- Omniscient: God is all-knowing. There is no limit to His

knowledge for He is the creator of all knowledge and truth (Job 37:16, Rom 11:33).

- Omnipresent: God is all-present: There is no limit to His presence. He is the God of heaven, hell and the universe, as we know it and more. He is everywhere present, dwelling with His creation, filling every point of space, but in no way bound by space. He is here with you (Psalm 139:7-12).
- Omnipotent and sovereign: God is all-powerful. There is no limit to His power for He is power. If anything has power, he, she or it, has power because God has given them power. Nothing frustrates God (Gen 18:14, Hos 11:9).
- Immutable (never changing): God is unchanging. Because He is perfect, He cannot become more perfect. And God is in this state, always good, always perfect, always loving and more. He was who He was when before He created the world and He the same today. (Psalm 90:2, Malach 3:6)
- Holy: God is entirely other. He is God and everything else is creation. Furthermore, God is entirely pure and entirely good, hating evil and hating sin (Habakkuk 1:13, Revelation 4:8; 15:4).
- Righteous and just: In all God does, He is righteous and just.

It is the holiness of God made manifest. It is for this reason God cannot do wrong. All He does is right. All He does is good (Deut 10:17, 32:4; Isaiah 9:7).

- Love: God is love. Any act of love points back to God for all love is from God It is for love that God humbled Himself and sacrificed Himself. Love was the motivation for the cross of Christ. God's love for us is the reason we even read this book. He saved us because He first loved us (John 3:16; 1 John 4:16, 19).

The purpose of studying God's attributes is not just so we can have theological knowledge about God. The purpose is to meditate on these attributes and to have your mind and heart completely renewed by God's awesomeness – to come to a point of profound worship, where we declare, "God, you are amazing! I can't wrap my mind around you, but I love you! I worship you! You are an awesome God!"

TAKE AWAYS: HEAD – HEART – HANDS

What has God revealed to you about Himself in this chapter? What are some things you struggle to believe about God? Are there behaviors or habits in your life that are rooted in not believing something about God? What has God revealed to you in these areas?

INTERCESSION

FOR YOURSELF

You are only able to know God as He reveals Himself to you. Pray through Ephesians 1:17, that the God of our Lord Jesus Christ, the Father of glory, may give you a spirit of wisdom and of revelation in the knowledge of Him.

FOR THE CHURCH

Pray for this coming Sunday's service and any other church meeting you have this week. In the spirit of Ephesians 1:17, continue to pray that God would give your church wisdom and revelation of Him, that in your meetings, it would not be routine, but it would be authentic worship of God in response to a greater revelation of Him.

FOR THE CITY

Pray for your city; that the churches in your city would be the revelation of God, both through their words and their actions. Pray for your churches to be missional in this way.

FOR THE NATIONS

The reason the church does missions to the nations is because so many countries do not know the goodness and glory of God. Ask God that He would reveal Himself to these countries through the missionaries and local churches. In addition, pray that God would reveal Himself in any way, whether through dreams and visions, or through tracts or media; that their eyes would be revealed to Jesus.

MEMORY VERSE

The LORD passed before him and proclaimed, "The LORD, the LORD, a God merciful and gracious, slow to anger, and abounding in steadfast love and faithfulness, keeping steadfast love for thousands, forgiving iniquity and transgression and sin.

– Exodus 34:6-7a

GOSPEL I: THE BIBLICAL STORY

Then he said to them, "These are my words that I spoke to you while I was still with you, that everything written about me in the Law of Moses and the Prophets and the Psalms must be fulfilled." Then he opened their minds to understand the Scripture. -Luke 24:44-45

An emaciated gospel leads to emaciated worship. It lowers our eyes from God to self and cheapens what God has accomplished for us in Christ. The biblical gospel, by contrast, is like fuel in the furnace of worship. The more you understand about it, believe it, and rely on it, the more you adore God both for who he is and for what he has done for us in Christ.

– Greg Gilbert

INTERACTION

Do you remember a time in your life when you heard good news? What was the news and how did you respond?

____

____

What does it mean for someone to become Christian?

INTRODUCTION

What is the gospel? The reason we are doing this study is because of the gospel. Churches are planted because of the gospel. Ministries try to be "gospel-centered". People even use the word "gospel" interchangeably with God, Jesus or the cross. But what does it mean?

The Greek word for "gospel" literally means good news. It comes in the context of battles and wars. The messenger would come riding to town with the gospel of victory, or good news of victory, to proclaim to the local people. It is from this context the word "gospel" has been derived in the Christian context.

INSTRUCTION

You came to know Christ by hearing the gospel. In this section, we want to expand your understanding of the gospel. Yes, Jesus loved you and died for you, but there is much more to it than that. In order for you to truly understand the good news of the gospel, you have to have a greater understanding of the bad news the gospel comes in light of. To do this, we must take a look at the greater storyline of the Bible.

The Bible can be understood in terms of four major divisions: creation, fall, redemption, and consummation. Let's take a look into each of these.

CREATION

Read Genesis 1 and 2. What happens in Genesis 1 and 2? Why do you think God gave us Genesis 1 and 2?

____

____

____

____

What do you learn about God?

What do you learn about creation?

What do you learn about the relationship between God and man?

FALL

Read Genesis 3 in light of Genesis 2:17. What happens in Genesis 3?

Summarize Genesis 3.

In what ways do we see sin's impact?

- Genesis 3:7 ______

- Genesis 3:8

- Genesis 3:12-13

- Genesis 3:17-18

- Genesis 3:24

In addition, we see the ravenous destructive nature of sin in the following chapters. Just one chapter later, a cold-blooded murder is committed. Cain murders his brother out of envy and jealously. Immediately, we see the absolute evil of sin. Then just a few chapters later, Genesis 6:5, 11-12 reveal the reality of what we cannot see in our hearts. What do we learn about sin's impact through these verses?

- Genesis 6:5

____

____

- Genesis 6:11-12

____

____

Sin always leads to death. Sin always leads to destruction. Sin is the very opposite of what God intended. God always desires for life to flourish. His very first commands were for man and woman to multiply and have dominion over the earth. Sin is everything that is not of God - and that was what had filled the hearts of man after the fall - for "every intention of the thoughts of his heart was only evil continually" (Genesis 6:5).

The New Testament further clarifies the wide and deep effects of sin. What do we learn about sin's effects through these verses?

- Romans 3:23

____

____

- Romans 6:23

____

____

What did we learn about sin? Summarize the evil effects of sin.

____

____

____

REDEMPTION

As someone reads Genesis 1-3, the reader's heart should break when realizing that this broken world that we see today was not always how it was. In fact, it was not what God had originally intended. Furthermore, the question should arise in the reader's mind, "Will the power and the effects of sin ruin things forever?", "What is going to happen with the relationship of God and man?", "Will it be marred forever?" And it is in this sad reality that the good news comes in.

In what ways do you see a glimpse of God's love and grace in the following verses.

- Genesis 3:15

____

____

- Genesis 3:21

____

____

We see that God has never stopped loving his people. Although He hates everything of sin, He still absolutely loves his people. We see that God is still good, gracious and compassionate. Furthermore, we see that God has a plan to crush Satan. Then, through the story of Abraham, in Genesis 12:1-3, we see a plan to bless all the nations.

The rest of the Old Testament is a story of redemption. Through Abraham, Isaac and Jacob, through Moses, the judges, the kings and the prophets, it leads to the ultimate redemption that is found in Jesus Christ. That is why Luke 24:44-45 says,

> *Then he said to them, "These are my words that I spoke to you while I was still with you, that everything written about me in the Law of Moses and the Prophets and the Psalms must be fulfilled. Then he opened their minds to understand the Scriptures."*

What is that redemption? And how does redemption come to us?

- John 3:16

____

____

- John 11:25-26

____

____

This is the heart of the gospel: God restores the relationship between God and man. Man is the most prized of all of creation. The main reason God desired to restore man is because He loves man. But this isn't the whole gospel.

"Who has truly pondered the weight of sin? The one who truly pondered the weight of the cross."

– Anselm of Canterbury

CONSUMMATION

When we think about the gospel, the first thing we think about is how God saved man. And appropriately so. However, what's so interesting about the gospel is that it doesn't end with man.

What else is being redeemed?

- Romans 8:19-21

  ____

  ____

- Rev 21:1

  ____

  ____

- Rev 21:4

  ____

  ____

When we read Revelation, we learn that its ends where everything began. We have a glimpse into the future and the future looks much like the past. God created this world perfectly and He intends to restore all of creation to its former glory. This is heaven! This is the purpose for which we have the gospel.

Things that you see or experience in this world will lead you to say, "This is NOT what life is supposed to be like!" or "This is not right!" Every time that happens, it is a reminder that this world is not heaven. Those who have tasted the brokenness of this world are those who long for heaven. Describe a time when you have felt this way.

____

____

____

____

C.S. Lewis writes,

> *"All the things that have ever deeply possessed your soul have been but hints of it -- tantalizing glimpses, promises never quite fulfilled, echoes that died away just as they caught your ear. But if it should really become manifest -- if there ever came an echo that did not die*

away but swelled into the sound itself -- you would know it. Beyond all possibility of doubt you would say "Here at last is the thing I was made for." [2]

There are times in life when we say, "This IS what life is supposed to be like!" or "This is what God meant life to be like!" These are all hints of the joy we will experience in heaven. What have been some moments in your life that hints forward to heaven?

___

___

___

___

We will one day live in a sinless world, truly loving God and loving each other, as originally intended. People will truly love each other.

There will be no more oppression, greed, apathy or hatred. Can you imagine what that will be like? It's hard to imagine, isn't it? But in our hearts, we crave to live this way and in this world. Furthermore, not only will we love each other, but our love for God will be pure.

2 C. S. Lewis, C. S.. *The Problem of Pain*. New York, NY: HarperOne, 2001.

I don't know about you, but I cannot wait to have that kind of unhindered intimacy with my Jesus.

John Piper writes,

> *"The critical question for our generation—and for every generation—is this: If you could have heaven, with no sickness, and with all the friends you ever had on earth, and all the food you ever liked, and all the leisure activities you ever enjoyed, and all the natural beauties you ever saw, all the physical pleasures you ever tasted, and no human conflict or any natural disasters, could you be satisfied with heaven, if Christ were not there?"*[3]

John 17:3 states, "And this is eternal life, that they know you the only true God, and Jesus Christ whom you have sent." You may not be able to know Him fully, in all His revealed glory, but you can know Him truly. As we close this chapter, meditate on how you have experienced God and what He means to you. Who is Jesus to you?

____

____

____

3 John Piper, *God Is the Gospel: Meditations on God's Love as the Gift of Himself*, Wheaton, IL: Crossway, 2005

TAKE AWAYS: HEAD – HEART – HANDS

What resonated with you most in this chapter of the gospel section?

How did this chapter expand your understanding of the gospel?

Does this fresh look at the gospel affect your head, your heart, or your hands? How so?

INTERCESSION

FOR YOURSELF

Thank the Lord for His endless pursuit of His people. As you have learned, the only reason the church exists today is not because we are so good, but because God is so good and He has chosen to pursue and save His people. We are the result of His grace. Thank Him!

FOR THE CHURCH

We have learned that the Bible is not so much about what we need to do for God, but what God has already done for us! The grand story of the Bible is the gospel story. It's important that the church understands that this is the Christian message. Christ came not because we were perfect, but actually for the very opposite reason; because we were imperfect. Pray for your church; that the focus will always be about what Christ has done for us, more so than what we are trying to do for God. All that we do, is simply a response to Him.

FOR THE CITY

The church is supposed to be a model of a heavenly community. As a result, it should to be an attractive community for people living in the city. In this way, the church should not only preach the gospel message but demonstrate the fruit of the gospel message. Pray that your church has a direct impact in the neighborhood and city it is in.

FOR THE NATIONS

It is unfortunate that Christianity is in the same category as other religions around the world. All the other religions say that you have to be good enough to be accepted by God. The Christian message is the very opposite. It says, "Because you are not good enough, God will provide a way for you to be accepted by God". Pray for the nations to truly hear and understand the pure message of justification by grace through the gospel message.

MEMORY VERSE:

For the wages of sin is death, but the free gift of God is eternal life in Christ Jesus our Lord. - Romans 6:23

GOSPEL II: REPENTANCE

For I am not ashamed of the gospel, for it is the power of God for salvation to everyone who believes, to the Jew first and also to the Greek. - Romans 1:16

When our Lord and Master Jesus Christ said "Repent," he intended that the entire life of believers should be repentance.
-Martin Luther

INTERACTION

What happens when one understands the gospel at an intellectual, emotional and spiritual level?

____

____

____

INTRODUCTION:

A picture is worth a thousands words. With technological advances in photography, it is easier to take breath-taking photos than ever before. With a stock lens on a DSLR camera, you can take a good quality photo of the Grand Canyon. But if you were to put on a wide-angle lens, you can take a wider, more full picture of the Grand Canyon that captures the glory more completely with one shot. In the previous chapter, as we looked at a broad scope of the gospel, it's like we took a wide-angle camera lens to the Bible to take a picture of the gospel.

In this chapter, our goal is to take 50mm lens and take a deep hard zoomed in picture of the gospel. Then we want to take a mirror and look at ourselves. Becoming a Christian and knowing how one becomes Christian are two different things. Taking a deeper look into the gospel will help us understand the dynamics of repentance which will enable us to strengthen our faith.

As we study the heart of repentance, we will notice that repentance is at the beginning of every believer's faith journey. But in addition, we will also see that repentance is the mark of the whole faith journey. In studying the gospel more deeply, we will see that repentance is a critical part of becoming a Christian and growing deeper as a Christian. It will solidify our faith and produce in us an assurance of salvation.

INSTRUCTION

When looking at the Bible with a wide-angle lens, it is very apparent what the Bible is about – it is about the story of God's pursuing love that provides a way to be with His people. We can break down the truth of the Bible to two main truths. First, God is holy, loving and good. Second, man is sinful, selfish and evil. With these truths, there is a great dilemma. How can a holy God dwell with sinful man? This is the question the Bible aims to answer. In light of this question, the Old Testament sets up the story for the coming of Jesus. The answer to the question is in the person and work of Jesus Christ.

Let's take a deeper look into understanding the gospel to learn how to respond to the gospel well. To do that, we will look at two different people and how they respond to Jesus.

Read Mark 10:17-22 and Luke 19:1-9.

Mark 10:17-22	Luke 19:1-9
How does the Rich man respond to the Jesus?	How does Zacchaeus respond to Jesus?
Why do you suppose He responds in such a way?	Why do you suppose He responds in such a way?
The way Jesus interacts with people is always very purposeful. In Mark 10:21, Jesus tells him to do the one thing He cannot do. Jesus knows full well that this is the one thing He cannot do. But we are told that the reason Jesus tells him to do such a thing is because He loved him. Why do you think Jesus would tell him to do the one thing He cannot do out of love? What do you think Jesus was trying to do?	In contrast, look at how Jesus interacts with Zacchaeus. Jesus spots him, pursues him and then invites Himself to Zacchaeus' home. Why does Jesus act so kindly to him? The answer is revealed in the text. How is Zacchaeus described throughout this passage? Verses 2, 3, 7 and 10.

Luke 19:10 says, For the Son of Man came to seek and to save the lost. Throughout the gospels, it is important to see how Jesus chooses to interact with people. Jesus acts very graciously towards those who know their sin. What He desires for them to know is that though they are sinners, God still loves them and He is the way to the Father. To those who are blind to their sin, Jesus, in his love, tries to reveal their sin.

It goes back to the two main truths of Scripture. God is holy. Man is sinful. To those that know their sin, He loves them by revealing to them that God is gracious. To those that do not know their sin, He loves them by revealing to them their sin. It is only when one knows that they need to be saved, that they will seek a savior. That is Jesus' goal. First, that man would know that they are a sinner. Second, that they know that Jesus is their savior.

So the question is, how will you respond? If you know you are a sinner, you will seek out a savior and repent. If you don't know you are a sinner, you will see no need for a savior and continue on with life.

What is your tendency? Are you often aware of your sins? Or are you often blind to your sin? We need to always be seeking to reflect and repent. Take sometime to write down the sins in your life. Be specific. As you do, thank Jesus for dying for these sins.

____

____

____

In addition, as we learned from the rich man, we are often blind to our sins. One of Jesus' ministries to us is to make us aware of our sin. This is what He did with the rich man in Mark 10. It is because He loves that He wants us to see our need for Him.

There are two main ways God makes us aware of our sin. First, through the work of the Holy Spirit, God will reveal to us hidden sins in our lives. Take some time to ask God to search your heart and to make you aware of your sin.

List what the Holy Spirit is revealing to you:

____

____

____

The second way God often reveals to us hidden sin is through the work of a brother or sister in Christ. Often times, those closest to us can see us better than we see ourselves. It is a healthy habit to ask those closest to us to tell us areas of sin and weakness in our lives. I know this can be a very scary thing to do, but as we do, God will purify us and make us more like Christ. Ask 2-3 people that know you best, what areas of sin they see in your life and areas of weakness where you need to grow. Ask them to be honest and share with you in love.

List what they shared:

____

____

____

WHAT HAPPENS IN REPENTANCE?

When Zacchaeus experienced the love of Christ, in essence, he repented. How? He wanted to make right his wrongs by giving to the poor and specifically paying back fourfold to those he defrauded. So we see repentance has some sort of action, but we want to take a deeper look into the components of repentance.

Look up the following verses as each reveals certain qualities about repentance.

- John 16:8; Rom. 3:20 (Knowledge and conviction of Sin)

____

____

- 2 Cor. 7:9 -10; Rom. 2:4 (Grief over past and present sin)

____

____

- Ezekiel 14:6; Acts 26:20 (Will to change)

____

____

- 1 Cor 1:18 (Rejoicing in the cross)

____

____

THE FRUIT OF A REPENTANT LIFE

It has been one of the greatest misunderstandings of the believer that the gospel is important for salvation, but unimportant for Christian living. It is a misconception that the gospel is about how to become a Christian, but not how to be a Christian. You will see that to live a Christian life does not mean to simply live a life of do's and don'ts, but to live a Christian life is to live a gospel-centered life. Summarize the passages below.

- Gal 1:6-7

____

____

- Gal 3:1-6

____

____

- Col 1:3-6

____

____

You see, the gospel is not the ABC's of Christianity, it is the A-Z of Christianity. The gospel is not just for salvation, but it is for sanctification. All of life is learning how deeply saved we have been from our sin.

FALSE REPENTANCE VS GOSPEL REPENTANCE

The idea of repentance is not unfamiliar in other religions. In the Jewish, Islam and Mormon faith, repentance is taught and practiced. However the way these religions practice repentance is entirely different to how Christians repent. You see, in every other religion, the reason and motivation to repent is to get right with God. If you sin, you confess and repent, so that you can live a life in which God will hopefully accept you. However, for the Christian, if you sin, the reason you confess and repent is because you have already been accepted by God, through the work of Jesus Christ. Christian repentance is Christ-centered, cross-driven, grace motivated.

You see, for the Christian, the reason you repent is because you are already in a relationship with God. Take a look at some characteristics of false repentance and gospel repentance below. As you look at the chart, ask yourself which category you fall into.

False Repentance	**Gospel Repentance**
False Repentance asks, "What must I do?"	Gospel Repentance asks, "What must God do? (What did God do?)"

False Repentance is concerned about "How will I live differently."	Gospel Repentance iscerned about "Why will I live differently?"
False Repentance is focused on action. • It says, "Fix yourself!" • False repentance kills. • False repentance sighs.	Gospel Repentance is focused on a person. (Jesus) • It says, "God save me" • Gospel repentance gives life. • Gospel repentance sings!
False repentance is self-centered. • We repent to keep God happy so that He will continue to bless us and answer our prayers. • We are sorry because of the consequences of sin in our lives. • It brings us punishment so we repent to avoid it. • We are sorry of the consequences of sin because we love ourselves. • False repentance starts with you and ends with you.	Gospel repentance is God-centered. • We repent to tap into the joy of our union with Christ in order to weaken our need to do anything contrary to God's heart. • We are sorry for the offense sin is to a holy God. • It displeases and dishonors Him. • We are sorry for the sin itself because we love God. • Gospel repentance starts at the cross and ends at the cross.

False repentance is centered upon self-righteousness. • We atone for our sins. • It is a form of self-flagellation in which we convince God (and ourselves) that we are so truly miserable and regretful that we deserve to be forgiven. • We earn our forgiveness with our repentance.	Gospel repentance is centered upon God's righteousness. • Christ atoned for our sins. • We received the forgiveness, because God forgives us because He is just. (1 John 1:8). It would be unjust to ever deny us forgiveness, because Jesus earned our acceptance! • We repent because we are forgiven. We just receive it.
False repentance is burdensome • Our hope is to live a good enough life for God to bless us. • We repent less and less.	Gospel repentance is joyful. • Our hope is that God lived a good enough life and in Christ, He blesses us. • We repent more and more.
False repentance has a cross, but you are crucified.	Gospel repentance has the cross, marked with blood, but it is empty. For Christ has risen.

When you pray and repent, do you finish with a grateful heart? Or are you more burdened?

____

____

May your repentance be Christ-focused, not self-focused. In doing so, your repentance will be an experience of stepping into deeper communion with the Lord as opposed to a guilt-ridden exercise.

TAKE AWAYS: HEAD – HEART – HANDS

What resonated with you most in this section on repentance? When you repent, is it focused on your sin or on Christ? Do you have joy when you repent? Or is your heart heavy?

INTERCESSION

FOR YOURSELF

Take some time to confess your sins, but as you do, thank Christ for the forgiveness you find in Him. Don't wallow in your sin, but learn to rejoice in the cross.

FOR THE CHURCH

May the church be a place where sinners come and find not judgment, but forgiveness and love. Pray for your church that it would become a place where if a prostitute came into your church, they would find grace and love, not judgment.

FOR THE CITY

Jesus came not for the healthy, but the sick. People will go to see the doctor only when they know they are sick. Pray for your city that people would be convicted of their sin and that this would lead them to find forgiveness in the cross.

FOR THE NATIONS

Many people are in bondage trying to get to heaven by mere performance. Whether one's a Muslim, Hindu, Buddhist, or of any other religion, if they were to be honest with their hearts, they would know that they still fall short before a perfect standard. Pray that God would bring a conviction of their sin and a greater conviction of the free salvation that is found in Jesus.

MEMORY VERSE

If we confess our sins, he is faithful and just to forgive us our sins and to cleanse us from all unrighteousness. -1 John 1:9

WORSHIP: RESPONDING TO HIS WORTH

"Ascribe to the Lord the glory due His name; worship the Lord in the splendor of holiness." Psalm 29:2

God is most glorified in us, when we are most satisfied in Him.
-John Piper

INTERACTION

When you hear the word "worship", what kinds of images come to mind?

____

____

____

____

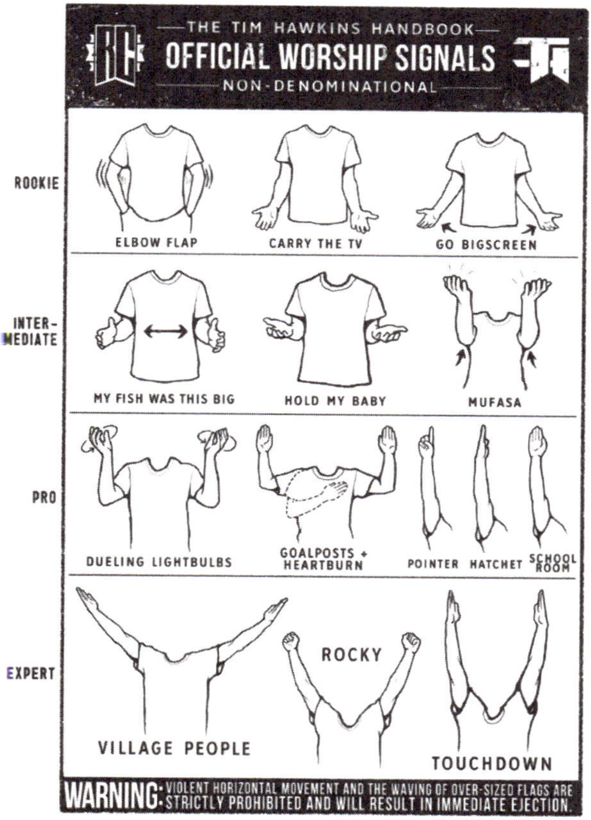

INTRODUCTION

Worship is central to what we do as Christians. The word worship is derived from the words "worth ship", meaning to declare the worth of the object being adored. John Piper defines it as "a way of gladly reflecting back to God the radiance of His worth." Many people think of worship and praise being the same thing. While praise (with singing and music) is part of worship, worship is much bigger and broader than just that. Worship is a part of life and an overflow into all areas of our lives. Worship is declaring His goodness by living for His glory. "So, whether you eat or drink, or whatever you do, do all to the glory of God." (1 Corinthians 10:31)

Part of learning to do all things to the glory of God comes from cultivating a life of worship, both in the private areas of our lives and the public. Worship is not just something we do on Sundays with our local church body, it is a daily part of putting God at the center of our days. While no list can be truly comprehensive in terms of how we can develop personal and corporate worship in our lives, in the next section, there is a list of foundational areas that can help us take steps in the right direction

INSTRUCTION

Worship begins with the Word of God. We know who the one true God is because He has revealed Himself to us through His Word. So for worship to be true, it must be grounded in Scripture. As discussed in the first chapter, one of the best habits to develop in cultivating a life of personal worship is having a daily quiet time with God.

RELATIONSHIP WITH GOD

Read these verses and observe what the person's relationship with God was described as:

Genesis 5:24

____

____

Genesis 6:9

____

____

SCRIPTURE

In chapter 1, we went over the importance of reading His Word. It is God's Word to us. It is vital to our sustenance. How has your time in the Word been? Think about your time in the Word since the first chapter and write down how your life is affected when you are in the Word and when you are not in the Word.

If you have been inconsistent in the Word, why have you been inconsistent? How do you view yourself or how do you view the Word in such a way that leads you to not be dependent on God and his Word?

PRAYER

Prayer at its core is communicating to God. It is a dialogue between us and God. Prayer is important because it allows us to share our concerns and desires with God. Though many struggle with prayer, we need to remember that it is something we learn and grow in. The disciples of Jesus even asked Him to teach them how to pray (Luke 11:1). So in this section we want to learn a little more of how we can develop our prayer lives.

What does Philippians 4:6-7 reveal about the role of prayer in our lives?

THE LORD'S PRAYER

Read Matthew 6:6-13

What does the Lord's prayer reveal about our relationship with God? Who are we to Him? And who is He to us?

What elements do you find in the Lord's prayer that model for us what we should also be praying for?

What do these verses say about our role in forgiveness? What connection is there between our lives (as we forgive) and prayer (as we ask for forgiveness)?

____

____

PRAYING THROUGH SCRIPTURE

Another way to develop your prayer life is to let Scripture be your teacher and guide. The Bible is filled with prayers and using those prayers to guide your own prayers is a wonderful way to mature the content of your praying.

THE PSALMS

From the heights of praise to the depths of pain, the Psalms provide a picture of what passion looks like in the place of prayer.

- Are you looking to express great praise to our God? Pray through Psalm 48.
- Are you stressed because of the suffering in the world around us? Pray through Psalm 46.
- Are you struggling with doubts and envy? Pray through Psalm 73.

- Try praying through Psalm 7 right now with your friend. Read through the Psalm together out load and then choose certain verses and turn them into your own prayer.
- If you have never done so before, try praying through one chapter of Psalms each day during your quiet times and your prayer life may never be the same again!

THE EPISTLES

Many of the letters (or epistles) written in the New Testament include prayers within them. This is another way to learn how to develop praying for other people and interceding for their needs.

Go through these prayers and take note of the things that Paul prays for concerning his brothers and sisters in these churches.

- 1 Corinthians 1:4-9 ______________________________

  ____
- Ephesians 1:15-23 ______________________________

  ____
- Philippians 1:3-11 ______________________________

  ____

- Colossians 1:3-14 ________________________________

____

THE ACTS MODEL

Another helpful pattern that can help balance our prayer lives is the "ACTS" model of prayer. Sometimes our prayers can be very heavily focused on asking God for things and we may neglect giving thanks to Him. Other times we may spend a great deal of time confessing our sins, but forget to give God praise for who He is. This "ACTS" model of prayer can help us keep a good balance in our prayers so that they don't become just one-sided. ACTS stands for: adoration, confession, thanksgiving, and supplication.

1. **Adoration:** declaring the goodness of God's character and praising His attributes.
   Psalm 145

2. **Confession:** honestly and humbly admitting our sins to God and turning away from them in repentance.
   1 John 1:9

3. **Thanksgiving:** expressing gratitude for the many ways that God has blessed our lives.

Psalm 100

4. **Supplication:** presenting our requests and needs before the Lord.

1 Peter 5:7; Philippians 4:6-7

FASTING

Fasting is giving up something good for the sake of something better. Jesus assumes that His disciples would fast in Matthew 6:16. While a fast would usually involve giving up food for a period of time, one could technically give up anything good during a fast. The way fasting becomes an expression of worship is that we are saying, "God, I choose to give up this good thing in order to have more focused time to seek after You." It is a hunger for more of God.

What does Mark 2:20 reveal about when His disciples would fast again?

____

Fasting is more than giving up something for yourself. It also includes caring for those in need around us. Read Isaiah 58 and take note of what other elements of fasting are required by God.

What connection does Isaiah 58 make between fasting and justice?

What is the warning of Jesus concerning fasting in Matthew 6:16-18. Why do you think this warning was given? Is it something to be careful of in our day and age as well? Share.

Besides food, what would be other things could you fast from?

____

____

____

NOTE: Please check with your doctor to make sure that fasting from food is safe for your health if you have never fasted before or if you plan on doing a fast for an extended period of time.

GIVING

Author Randy Alcorn once said, "We often think we own our possessions, but too often they own us." Giving can be one of the clearest expressions of worship because we are showing that what we value most is God more than our bank accounts. It is an act of worship because we are also showing where we put our trust. Those who realize that everything we have is from God and for God, are able to give generously.

How do you spend your money? On a scale of 1-10 (10 being generous), where would you rate yourself? Why?

____

____

What is a hurdle you have in the way you handle your money?

____

____

____

What is the warning given in 1 Timothy 6:10?

____

____

____

How does tithing become an expression of our trust in God?

____

____

____

Read Philippians 4:14-20. What does this passage reveal about God's view of our giving?

____

____

____

What does 1 Timothy 6:17-19 teach us about where we need to put our hope?

____

____

____

In your own words, summarize how our giving is connected to our worship? How can you better worship God through your finances?

____

____

____

TAKE AWAYS: HEAD – HEART – HANDS

What struck you most about this chapter on Worship? Was this a new lesson or revelation, or a reminder of a lesson/revelation you have had in the past? What do you think it means to "walk with God?" What would it look like to "walk with God" throughout your day?

INTERCESSION

FOR YOURSELF

Worship is not just something that is done through songs at church. Worship is living in light of the worth of God. We worship because He is worthy. Ask God to continue to open your eyes to see and experience His glory.

FOR THE CHURCH

Pray for your Sunday service. Pray for the praise time that it would lead to see and experience the majesty of God. Pray for your pastor that through the preached word, the congregation would understand in a greater capacity His supreme worth. May it lead your church to a life or worhsip.

FOR THE CITY

Pray for the churches in your city; that the worship given to God on Sunday and the worship lived out throughout the week would be stronger, louder and more passionate than any worship given to any local sports team or celebrity. Christ is better and greater!

FOR THE NATIONS

John Piper once said, "Missions exist because worship does not." The reason we do missions is because God is not worshipped in other nations and that the greatest injustice. Pray that the life of the church in all the nations would be a beautiful picture of the worth of Christ so that more would join us in our worship of the King.

MEMORY VERSE

Teach me your way, O LORD, that I may walk in your truth;
unite my heart to fear your name.
I give thanks to you, O Lord my God, with my whole heart,
and I will glorify your name forever. -Psalm 86:11-12

COMMUNITY: LIFE IN THE BODY

Though I speak with the tongues of men and of angels, but have not LOVE, I have become sounding brass or a clanging symbol. though I have the gift prophecy, and understand all mysteries and all knowledge, and though I have all faith, so that I could remove mountains, but have not LOVE, I am nothing. though I bestow all my goods to feed the poor and though I give my body to be burned, but have not love, it profits me nothing. - 1 Corinthians 13:1-3

"Christian community is like the Christian's sanctification. It is a gift of God which we cannot claim. Only God knows the real state of our fellowship, of our sanctification. What may appear weak and trifling to us may be great and glorious to God. Just as the Christian should not be constantly feeling his spiritual pulse, so, too, the Christian community has not been given to us by God for us to be constantly taking its temperature. The more thankfully we daily receive what is given to us, the more surely and steadily will fellowship increase and grow from day to day as God pleases."

-Dietrich Bonhoeffer, Life Together

INTERACTION

What is the best community you have been a part of? Why was it good?

____

____

What is your community like at church?

____

____

INTRODUCTION

I was sitting in a café and as I looked up, I saw 5 people walking down the street together. It was clear they knew each other by how close they were walking near each other. But something was peculiar and I couldn't put my finger on it at first. As I continued to observe their interaction, I was able to figure out what was off. What was interesting about their interaction was actually their lack of interaction. From one end of the street to the other, they did not speak one word with each other. The whole time, they were looking down on their phones.

This is a picture of a false community. False community takes place when there are superficial benefits of connectedness without the genuine and deep interactions of connectedness that people have a profound craving and need for. Due to the false communities that are prevalent today, people find themselves filling the void of deep relationships with more and more superficial interactions. These superficial interactions are characterized by conversations that never go to the deepest parts of our heart. These interactions are further reinforced by the advance of social media, such as Facebook, Instagram or even texting. These are real interactions but do not penetrate to the deeper parts of our hearts where we do life. Sherry Turkle observed that "we're designing technologies that will give us the illusion of companionship without the demands of friendship." [4]

False communities have led people to believe they are in community and subsequently, have misled people to not realize they are at the core, very lonely. As a generation, we have gone numb at our core. This is dangerous. Jessica Olien, journalist for the Medical Examiner writes, "Loneliness is not just making us sick, it is killing us. Loneliness is a serious health risk. Studies of elderly people

4 http://www.ted.com/talks/sherry_turkle_alone_together.html#727000

and social isolation concluded that those without adequate social interaction were twice as likely to die prematurely." [5] This is a problem because, "Loneliness has doubled: 40 percent of adults in two recent surveys said they were lonely, up from 20 percent in the 1980s." More and more people feel lonelier than ever before.

Community isn't just necessary on a social level. Community is necessary for the health and growth of an individual on a holistic level. This is reason the church is called to be a community. God designed us for community and the church is called to live a community. Therefore, we must not simply bring the pattern of how community is done in the world and adopt it into the church. We must look into scripture and learn to purposefully do community in a way that is drastically different to the world. Let's take a look into what the Bible reveals to us about the importance and role of community.

---

5 http://www.slate.com/articles/health_and_science/medical_examiner/2013/08/dangers_of_loneliness_social_isolation_is_deadlier_than_obesity.html

INSTRUCTION

IMPORTANCE OF LOVE

I know of a man who knows the Bible inside and out. You can read a few verses from any part of the Bible and he is able to name, within a few chapters, where those verses are from. His knowledge of the Bible is amazing. He is an excellent preacher and considered a great leader. When talking with someone who worked with him at a church, I was so excited to hear more about how much of a blessing it would be to work with him. He went on and on about how wise and skilled this man was. His ability to plan, execute and answer questions was inspiring. But what he said next was shocking. He said, "Having said all of that, I hated working for him." I was shocked. He clarified that he had learned a lot about theology, preaching and even leadership, but that he and many of the other people that worked for this man felt exactly the same way. That they only worked for him, but not with him. They felt that though he was so knowledgeable and skilled that at the end of his time, the man was a clanging cymbal.

The sign of a healthy growing believer is not necessarily Bible knowledge or skill, but it is love.

Read 1 Corinthians 13:1-3. What do you learn about love here?

Read 1 Corinthians 13:11 in the context of love. What would be considered childish ways or childish thoughts? What would be considered giving up these childish ways and becoming a man?

COMMUNITY IS ABSOLUTELY NECESSARY FOR LIFE

In the section about the gospel, we learned that God is good and that God created creation as good. In this section, we want to look into the creation story, and this time, let's take a deeper look at what is revealed concerning relationships.

Read Genesis 2:18-24. This passage reveals God's intentions for marriage, but more fundamentally, it reveals God's intentions for relationships. What can we learn about relationships even before sin had tainted relationships and how we do relationships?

What do we learn about God's relationship with man?

What do we learn about man's relationship with animals?

What do we learn about man's relationship with man?

COMMUNITY IS ABSOLUTELY NECESSARY FOR GROWTH

God created us to be in community. However, it would be a mistake to say that the goal of a Christian is to be in community. As we look into Scripture, we will see that being in community is more of a by-product of who we are in Christ and the purpose we have in Christ. It is in our deep and passionate pursuit of loving God and loving our neighbor that healthy communities are formed.

Jerry Bridges writes, "Biblical community is first of all the sharing of a common life in Christ."[6] Bridges quotes J.I. Packer, "Fellowship with God, then, is the source from which fellowship among Christians springs; and fellowship with God is the end to which Christian fellowship is a means."

How do the following verses further develop this thought.

What is the correlation we have in Christ and with each other in 1 John 1:3 and Romans 12:5?

____

____

Read the following verses. What is the lens through which Paul sees these people and these relationships?

6 Bridges, Jerry (2012-09-14). True Community: The Biblical Practice of Koinonia (Kindle Location 112). Navpress. Kindle Edition.

- Romans 16:3 ____

____

- 1 Corinthians 1:2 ____

____

- Ephesians 1:1-2 ____

____

- Philippians 1:1 ____

____

What is the purpose of relationships for Paul? What does this reveal about how we need to view our relationships?

____

____

____

How does the world often view relationships or the purpose of relationships?

____

We are called to be communities driven by love, not driven or paralyzed by fear. 1 John 4:18 says "There is no fear in love, but perfect love casts out fear. For fear has to do with punishment, and whoever fears has not been perfected in love." John is pointing out that as children of God, dearly loved, we should have no fear of judgment day because God loves us. So He calls believers to respond with love, not fear! In this, John reveals an important dynamic in relationships. What God desires from his children is not a fear driven relationship, but a love driven relationship. He desires his children to be secure in God's love so that we respond with love. This reveals that it is utterly vital for relationships to be driven by love not fear. And in the same way, He calls his children to have relationships driven by love, not fear. But these relationships are secure not because of man's love for us, but again because of God's love for us. 1 John 4:11-12 says, "Beloved, if God so loved us, we also ought to love one another. No one has ever seen God; if we love one another, God abides in us and his love is perfected in us." But so often, we are driven by fears in our relationships. These fears are rooted in selfish motives, often a fear of rejection.

What fears do you have in relationships that paralyze your ability to love?

____

____

____

____

____

WHAT DO LOVE-DRIVEN RELATIONSHIPS LOOK LIKE?

Read Acts 2:42-47. Write down observations of what a secure love-driven community acts like.

____

____

____

____

Read 1 Samuel 18:1-4. What do you learn about love-driven relationships?

____

As you read the following verses, ask God to reveal to you how your relationships have been driven by fear and selfishness, as opposed to others-centered love. In these verses, you will also see a contrast between self-driven relationships and others-driven relationships.

Romans 1:28-30 ______________________________

2 Corinthians 12:19-20 ______________________________

Galatians 5:19-21 ______________________________

Colossians 3:12-14 ______________________________

What would it look like if the question you asked yourself was not, "What can I get from them?" but "What can I give to them?" If the focus came off of you and went on the other person, what would your relationships look like?

____

____

____

____

____

____

ON MISSION TOGETHER

We do community because we are all of Christ. You are my brother or sister. As a community, together, we are on mission together. This will be developed more in the following sessions. But as we strive to love God, love one another and as we join God's mission to tell the world about Jesus, we need each other to be able to accomplish this. What do the following verses teach us about why we need each other?

Hebrew 3:13 ____________________________________

Hebrew 10:24 ______________________________

BOAST IN THE CROSS TOGETHER.

When we meet each other, we want to keep it centered on the cross. We can do that by confessing before God, and each other, our sins, so that we can boast of the cross. We may commit the same sin repeatedly, but have faith in God that as we confess our sins, He is faithful and just to forgive us and every time we confess, He purifies us. Every time we confess, He hears us and changes us. There is much grace in confession. As you confess your sins, take the focus off of yourself and focus on the cross. It is in Jesus that you find confidence in your forgiveness.

Furthermore, confess your sins to each other. Why? Isn't it enough that we confess our sins to God? It depends. In terms of being forgiven, confessing to God is sufficient. But in order to change and grow, it is not sufficient. When we confess our sins to one another, the evil of the sin is exposed bringing deeper conviction of sin and a greater reality of the gospel. Hence, James 5:16 exhorts believers to confess to each other and then pray for each other.

FIGHT TOGETHER

Hebrews 3:12-14 guides believers to be aware of unbelief and the deceitfulness of sin. The reason we commit sin is because of unbelief and deceitfulness. As you confess your sins, you want to take the next step and address the unbelief and deceit in your hearts that led you to commit the sins. As you do, strength and motivation will well up in you to fight again. In order to have a better understanding of our hearts and why we commit the sins that we do, ask each other questions. Why did you commit that sin? In what ways did you not believe in God and his ways? What lies have you believed to lead you to commit that sin? As you start to see the deeper motives and reasons for why you sin, you will be able to confess and repent more deeply.

WORSHIP TOGETHER

In Ephesians 5:18-20, what does Paul tell the church to do?

Did you know that as we worship God together, the act of being in the presence of fellow believers worshipping Him strengthens us? This is why we are called to actually speak and sing to God, and as we do, to also address each other. In doing so, we will encourage each other. How can you worship God together?

ADDITIONAL QUESTIONS TO ASK EACH OTHER

Here are some more questions to ask as you do life together for the sake of Christ. Remember, the reason we ask questions and share is because we are running this race together. Here are a few practical tips as you look to be in community to take steps of maturity.

1) Your discussion must not highlight or focus on the sin more than the finished work of Christ and the grace he gives us for that moment to repent and grow. 2) This is not a time to compare our "righteousness" or simply talk about our actions or lack their of. We

are always aiming to get to the relational and heart level. 3) A list of questions is insufficient for accountability. There is no perfect set of questions. And so ask each other, "How can I help you?" May your relationships be driven by love and grace, not fear and shame!

The following questions are taken from Jonathan Dodson's *Gospel-Centered Discipleship.*[7]

- What do you desire more than anything else?
- What do you find yourself daydreaming or fantasizing about?
- What lies do you subtly believe that undermine the truth of the gospel?
- Are you astonished with the gospel?
- Where have you made much of yourself and little of God?
- Is technology interrupting your communion with God?
- Is work a source of significance? How?
- Where do your thoughts drift when you enter a social setting?

7 Dodson has taken these questions from Sam Storms's book, A Sincere and Pure Devotion to Christ and David Powlison's list of "X-ray Questions. Sam Storms, A Sincere and Pure Devotion to Christ: 100 Daily Meditations on 2 Corinthians (Wheaton, IL: Crossway, 2010), 193–94. Dodson, Jonathan K. (2012-03-31). Gospel-Centered Discipleship (Re:Lit). 155. Crossway. Kindle Edition.

- What fears keep you from resting in Christ?
- What consumes your thoughts when you have alone time?
- When people see how you spend money, do they conclude that God is a priceless treasure, exceedingly valuable above all worldly goods?
- When people observe your relationship with others, are they alerted to the power of Christ's forgiveness of you that alone accounts for your forgiveness of them?
- If you are complimented for some accomplishment, does the way you receive it drive onlookers to give thanks to the Lord?
- Is your use of leisure time or devotion to a hobby or how you speak of your spouse the sort that persuades others that your heart is content with what God is for you in Christ?
- Does your reaction to bad news produce in you doubt or fear, or does it inspire confidence to trust in God's providence?

See Appendix for addition questions for accountability.

TAKE AWAYS: HEAD – HEART – HANDS

Community is vital for our faith. We are created for community. In what ways do you lack community? Furthermore, in what ways do others need you? Do you have one or two people who can ask the most difficult questions to love you and keep you accountable?

INTERCESSION

FOR YOURSELF

Do you have a same-gendered friend that you can closely do life together with? If so, pray for that person now. If not, ask God to bring someone into your life that you can do life together with.

FOR THE CHURCH

Pray for your church that it would be a true community where people are loving each other and passionately pursuing Christ together. Pray against any counterfeit aspects of community that may be present in your church.

FOR THE CITY

Pray for the people in your city that are in search of communities to find a true community in your church. As they are frustrated with their present communities, may your church be the community that they have been searching for.

FOR THE NATIONS

Pray for your missionaries in different countries. One of the greatest struggles missionaries have is fighting loneliness and feeling forgotten. Pray for your missionaries that God would comfort them and for God to provide brothers/sisters for them to fight together with.

MEMORY VERSE

And let us consider how to stir up one another to love and good works, not neglecting to meet together, as is the habit of some, but encouraging one another, and all the more as you see the Day drawing near. –Hebrew 10:24-2

DISCIPLESHIP: FOLLOWING HIM

And Jesus said to them, "Follow me, and I will make you become fishers of men." -Mark 1:17

Christianity without discipleship is always Christianity without Christ.

-Dietrich Bonhoeffer

INTERACTION

What does it mean to follow Jesus?

____

____

____

What did you leave behind to follow Jesus?

____

____

____

INTRODUCTION

Jesus equated faith with following Him to become His disciple. That means, in the language of His day, giving up everything to follow Jesus in His ministry – giving up home, family, comforts, sense of security, everything – in order to go wherever He goes and to participate in whatever ministry He does. Just as His disciples left everything to follow Him, we give up everything to spend our lives with Him, to learn from Him, his teaching and his lifestyle, and in turn learn to teach and minister to others.

That describes not only saving faith, but our daily practical faith. Trusting God in your daily relationship with Him means not only believing what He says, who He is, or what He will do. It means continuing to give up everything as you follow Him as His disciple. It means continuing to be fully committed to Him every day - giving Him everything, giving yourself fully to Him, and trusting Him fully for everything. That kind of faith changes us, and produces real fruit. We demonstrate this not in our ability to intellectualize about our faith, but in our hearts. We show it by loving God passionately, and by being visible disciples as Jesus called us to be.

Giving up everything to follow Jesus is no small thing. We can't be part-time disciples, or partially follow Him when we feel like it. Being His disciple means full commitment and obedience. That means rejecting worldly things like sin and temptation that would distract and hinder us from completely following Him.

Jesus' final words in Matthew add more to this biblical imperative of discipleship. The Great Commission (Matthew 28:16-20) tells us that being a disciple of Jesus means to trust that Christ has complete authority and in that authority, to go and share the gospel, to disciple others, and to teach them to obey also. So we need a proper biblical understanding of obedience. Obedience is not primarily about following a lot of rules. Obedience is about following Jesus.

In this chapter we'll talk about living as disciples, in terms of obedience and being part of a discipling community, where we get mentored and mentor others, directly and indirectly. In order to talk about obedience, we also have to talk about sin, temptation, spiritual warfare, and God's will.

INSTRUCTION

OBEDIENCE

Read James 1:13-26. What is obedience? Is it just doing or not doing certain things?

____

____

What does James say is the relationship between faith and works?

____

____

In which particular areas of your life do you find it harder to obey

Family	
Friends	
Romantic Relationships	
Money	
Work	
Life goals, dreams	
Status	
Other	

What is your motivation for obedience to God? What is competing with your godly motivation?

Look at the story of Mary and Martha in Luke 10:38-42. What insights do you gather about devotion to Jesus and works for Jesus?

Deep down in her heart, what might have been Martha's motivation for being preoccupied with all her busywork? In contrast, what was Mary's motivation for being with Jesus?

In a sense, obeying God is something that we do because we have to, since He does command us to do certain things. But ultimately, what is your motivation for serving Christ? For going to church? For serving in the church?

____

____

____

Christians sometimes go to extremes of legalism (rule based spirituality, where one ultimately relies on one's own strength), and libertinism (using God's grace and forgiveness as excuses for sin). How can you find the proper scriptural balance?

____

____

____

Ultimately, obedience is not about doing things because we have to, but because we want to. There should not be a conflict between faith and obedience in following Christ. Obedience is ultimately a matter of our hearts, as it is a natural result of our commitment and devotion to Christ – our love of Jesus, and our faith in Him. If we truly love Him, then we naturally want to do the things He wants us to do. Obedience is a natural result of our faith. If we have a passionate, active faith in Christ that produces a natural obedience, then it is easier to discern and follow God's will for our lives.

____

____

____

GOD'S WILL

Part of God's will is His moral will for our lives, and Scripture provides a number of guidelines for our obedience to God's will in how we live. This is part of His ultimate will and purpose for our lives, which is to be conformed to the image of Christ (Romans 8:29), and to be like Christ (2 Corinthians 3:18, 1 John 3:2-3), so that we can enjoy intimate fellowship with our God.

As we are called to be his disciples, we will struggle with what God's will is for our lives and for important decisions. Does God want me to serve Him by choosing this career or something else? By marrying a particular person? By taking a job at a particular company? By entering full-time ministry, or by being a witness in the secular marketplace? These and many other questions will test you throughout your life, but God's purpose in all this is for you to seek and find His will.

Sometimes God's will is crystal clear, especially on moral matters and making Him our number one priority in our lifestyle and decisions. In some matters we decide, but in accordance with the principles of God's kingdom. And sometimes God's Spirit reveals His will for specific decisions and callings, by speaking to us in various ways. For example, when it comes to marriage, Scripture clearly says that a single person should not choose to marry a non-believer (2 Corinthians 6:14). But a single person can choose which fellow believer to marry. God is not a magical matchmaker, who will choose someone that you "have to" marry. He will likely allow you to cross paths with a number of people, but choosing to marry one of those persons should be based on kingdom values, such as "Is this person a very godly, spiritually serious Christian?", "Will this be the kind of person I want to raise and disciple my children?", and "Do we have compatible life goals and ministry goals?"

In other matters, the Holy Spirit may speak to you in different ways. He may place a burden on your heart, He may give you a calling or conviction about something, He may open or close doors of opportunity, He may speak to you through His Word, He may communicate to you as you pray, and He may even occasionally communicate to you through signs or other supernatural means. Finding God's will is never easy, and it may not work the same way every time for every person. There is no simple formula for finding God's will. This is because He wants you to seek Him first (Matthew 6:32). He does not want us to treat Him like a magic answer machine that we come to (only or primarily) when we need help. He always wants us to depend on Him, seek Him, grow closer to Him, and wait on Him, before He reveals His will to us.

What does Romans 12:1-2 say about finding God's will?

In what areas are you seeking His will in your life? How does God reveal His will? That is, what happens first before He can reveal His will to you, and why?

What is His will for your life, at least right now?

SIN AND TEMPTATION

God says, "Be holy, for I am holy" (Leviticus 20:26, 1 Peter 1:16). This is not because God wants us to be religious robots, or because He is an arbitrary or mean God who doesn't want us to be happy. Rather, it is because God wants to have fellowship with us, and for us to be close to Him – because He desires spiritual intimacy with us. The more we let Him purify us, the closer we can come to Him.

What does 'holy' mean? What does it mean for us to be holy? What are the biggest obstacles to holiness in your life? (Be specific.)

Reflecting on what we learned in the chapter on the Gospel, summarize your understanding of sin and its consequence.

____

____

____

How do we handle temptation? Explain what the following principles mean.

- James 1:13-15 ______________________________

  ____

- James 4:7-8 ________________________________

  ____

- 1 Corinthians 10:12-13__________________________

  ____

What's your biggest challenge to holiness? What might that "way out" or escape route look like for you in your situation?

____

____

How do we deal with sin when we do commit it? What do these terms mean?

- Confession (1 John 1:9) ______________________________

____

- Repentance (Psalm 51:1-3) ___________________________

____

What are preventive measures for avoiding sin and temptation? See Psalm 119:11 and 119:105. What principle does this teach? According to these verses, why do we learn and memorize Scripture?

This is not just about avoiding temptation and sin (negative action), but about focusing our hearts on God (positive action). What are some other things that you can do to focus on God and avoid the distractions of temptation?

____

____

____

TAKE AWAYS: HEAD – HEART – HANDS

What struck you most about this chapter on discipleship? Was this a new lesson or revelation, or a reminder of a lesson you have had many times? What would it look like to walk with God throughout your day?

INTERCESSION

FOR YOURSELF

To follow Christ means to deny oneself. It is not easy to deny your desires. Remember, we deny ourselves for someone who is greater and someone who will truly satisfy us. Whatever struggles you have, lay it down before the Lord. If you have sins, confess it to the Lord. Ask the Lord to help you see that God is trustworthy, worthy and good.

FOR THE CHURCH

What God desires are followers of Christ – not Sunday spectators attending a worship service. He desires men and women who are obeying all that Christ had commanded. Pray for your church, that as a community, you would grow together to learn the teachings and obey the teachings of Christ.

FOR THE CITY

Pray for neighboring churches in your city. Pray for the believers in your city and any specific temptation or sin that would be specific to your city. For example, your city may be more inclined to sins related to poverty, sexual immorality, political corruption, work as idolatry, modern day slavery, sex-trafficking, orphans, neglect or idolatry of family, and others.

FOR THE NATIONS

Pray that God would raise up more disciples in all the nations. Pray for specific missionaries and churches to raise up local native disciples that will reach their fellow brothers and sisters.

MEMORY VERSES

And Jesus came and said to them, "All authority in heaven and on earth has been given to me. Go therefore and make disciples of all nations, baptizing them in the name of the Father and of the Son and of the Holy Spirit, teaching them to observe all that I have commanded you. And behold, I am with you always, to the end of the age.

– Matthew 28:18-20

SERVICE: AN ACT OF LOVE

If I then, your Lord and Teacher, have washed your feet, you also ought to wash one another's feet. For I have given you an example, that you also should do just as I have done to you. Truly, truly, I say to you, a servant is not greater than his master, or is a messenger greater than the one who sent him. If you know these things, blessed are you if you do them.

– John 13:14-17

The first question which the priest and the Levite asked was: "If I stop to help this man, what will happen to me?" But the good Samaritan reversed the question: "If I do not stop to help this man, what will happen to him?"

– Martin Luther King Jr

INTERACTION

In this chapter, you will see that serving others is a critical characteristic of a Christian. Are there ways in which you are serving others? If so, list them below.

What do you think is the purpose of serving others? How does it affect you when you serve?

INTRODUCTION

Picture a martian. As soon as you read the word, "martian," which color immediately came to mind? Most people visualize a green being of sorts. Over half a century of pop culture has imbedded this image of green martians with bulging eyes in our minds. And so the color green has become a defining characteristic of martians to us.

As Christians, what would be some of our main characteristics? The word "Christian" basically means "belonging to Christ," or "follower of Christ." So as followers of Christ, our lives should be marked with the same virtues Christ displayed and taught. If that is true, then this means we should live in the form of servants, as Christ did.

In his book *Multiply*, Francis Chan says that, "While every individual needs to obey Jesus's call to follow, we cannot follow Jesus as individuals."[8] This is why the Apostle Paul calls Christians together as the body of Christ (Rom. 12:5; 1 Cor. 12-27; Eph. 3:6; 5:23; Col. 1:18, 24). And as one body, "What matters is your interaction with the people God has placed in your life. If you are not connected with other Christians, serving and being served, challenging and being challenged, then you are not living as He desires, and the church is not functioning as He intended."[9]

INSTRUCTION

Writer James C. Wilhoit points out that Christians are "formed to serve [and] formed by serving."[10] As it says in Galatians 2:20, we must remember that it is no longer we who live, but Christ who lives in us. And as we live this life in the flesh by faith in the Son of God,

8 Francis Chan and Mark Beuving. *Multiply: Disciples Making Disciples*, p. 51.

9 Ibid., p. 52.

10 Wilhoit. *Spiritual Formation*, p. 149.

who loved us and gave Himself for us, service is what we are called to, and what will continue to grow us into the image of Christ. Our service will be a defining characteristic that will truly form us as Christians.

Which biblical passages or images can you think of after reading the previous paragraph?

____

____

Jesus intended for His followers to do as He has done for us throughout His ministry – be people who serve each other (Luke 22:24-27; John 13:14:17). We are "formed to serve." [11] The default posture or stance of a Christian is service. To serve is to have the same mind, the same love, and to be of one mind with Christ (Phil. 2:2-8).

The posture and attitude of service neither comes easily nor naturally to us – even as Christians. As Jesus Himself pointed out in Luke 22:27, human nature wants to be served rather than to serve.

11 James C. Wilhoit. *Spiritual Formation as if the Church Mattered: Growing in Christ through Community*, p. 149

The world today, as in Jesus' day, loves to follow the idea of a pecking order, where "those who are considered rulers ... lord it over [people], and exercise authority over them" (Mark 10:42). But Jesus goes on to say that "but it shall not be so among you." This is especially powerful because the society and culture of Jesus' day had a very structured and strict social ranking system. Status was publically recognized and honored.[12] In such a context, Jesus challenges the great to be servants: "Whoever would be first... must be slave of all. For even the Son of Man came not to be served but to serve, and to give his life as a ransom for many" (Mark 10:43-45). The Apostle Paul follows the standard set by Jesus, avoiding "the terms 'leader' or 'leadership' with reference to Christian communities, preferring to speak rather of service or ministry and co-workers."[13] We are clearly called to service.

List some real life examples of pecking orders in action and people lording over others. Discuss why you feel it occurs.

____

____

12 Andrew D. Clarke. Serve *the Community of the Church: Christians as Leaders and Ministers,* p. 249.

13 Ibid. P. 249.

Richard Foster wrote the following on the discipline of service: "In service we must experience the many little deaths of going beyond ourselves. Service banishes us to the mundane, the ordinary, the trivial." [14] And just as we are "formed to serve," we are "formed by serving." [15] Nothing teaches and forms humility in us like service. In serving, we surrender our need and desire to be "the greatest."

We see this in Luke 22:24: "A dispute also arose among [the disciples], as to which of them was to be regarded as the greatest." [16] It was this very issue that Jesus addressed in John 13:1-20, when He washed the feet of all the disciples as they gathered for the Passover Feast. The disciples were aware of the need for someone to wash their feet, but this was the job of servants or slaves, or the least in any group. [17] But Jesus stood up, grabbed a washbasin and a towel, then got on His knees to wash the disciples' dirty feet. Jesus is telling us to do the same. The Greek word, diakonia, often translated to "ministry" in English was "commonly associated with serving at tables" and other "menial and undignified contexts." [18] Jesus made a

14 Richard J. Foster. *Celebration of Discipline: The Path to Spiritual Growth*, p. 126-127.

15 Wilhoit, p. 149

16 See also Luke 9:46; Mark 10:41; Matt. 20:24

17 Foster, *Celebration of Discipline*, p. 126.

18 Andrew D. Clarke. *Serve the Community of the Church: Christians as Leaders and Ministers*, p. 235.

direct reference to this image in Luke 22:27 – that He did not come to be served while He reclined at the table, but as one who serves at the table. Jesus showed us what Philippians 2:6-7 looks like in the most practical sense, and still calls us to do as He did, in humility:

> *Who, being in very nature God,*
>> *did not consider equality with God something to be used to his own advantage;*
>> *rather, he made himself nothing*
>> *by taking the very nature of a servant,*
>> *being made in human likeness.*

With John 13:1-20 and Philippians 2:1-11 in front of you, try to list as many observations as you can of how Jesus personified humility. Please take your time with this and see how many you can write down.

____

____

____

____

____

In *Spiritual Formation as if the Church Mattered* James Wilhoit said that, "All Christians are called to worship God, utilize their gifts, and minister to others according to God's principles as set forth in Scripture."[19] Besides being a "place" where followers of Christ can interact with each other towards mutual growth, the church, or body of Christ is also intended to function as a place of learning and training. As Wilhoit points out, "Too often new Christians are slow to engage in areas of unique service because they feel inadequate."[20] One of the biggest responsibilities of pastors and the church is to teach and help believers fully realize their unique contribution in the Kingdom of God.

Taken from Saddleback Church, our ministry also offers the S.H.A.P.E. course to help our members find their "sweet-spot" to maximize their potential in serving and building the Kingdom of God. S.H.A.P.E. is an acronym that stands for Spiritual gifts, Heart, Abilities, Personality, and Experiences.

The expression of your S.H.A.P.E. is "your specific contribution to the body of Christ, within your generation, that causes you to totally depend on God and authentically

19 Wilhoit. P. 152.

20 Ibid. P. 150

display His love towards others." [21]

If you are not completely

sure of your "shape,"

consider signing up.

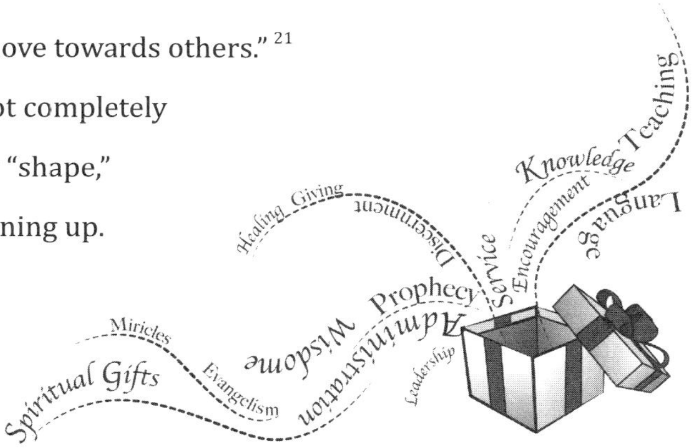

Do you know what your spiritual gifts are?

What are some things you are passionate about?

21 Erik Reese. S.H.A.P.E.: Finding and Fulfilling Your Unique Purpose for Life.

What are 3 abilities you are good at and love doing that others cannot do easily? Have you thought about something you are good at doing but you do not enjoy doing?

How would you describe your personality? What are some standout qualities about your personality?

Think about and discuss how a past experience, positive or negative, has shaped you to be the person you are today.

If you had difficulty answering some of the above questions or they triggered some urge to explore deeper, please consider signing up for the S.H.A.P.E. course.

As you think about your history of service and ministry in the church, take some time to discuss what Richard Foster calls, "Self-righteous service versus true service" [22] summarized in the following table. If you are serving in any capacity, discuss how your service can become self-righteous, and what kind of effort it takes for them to

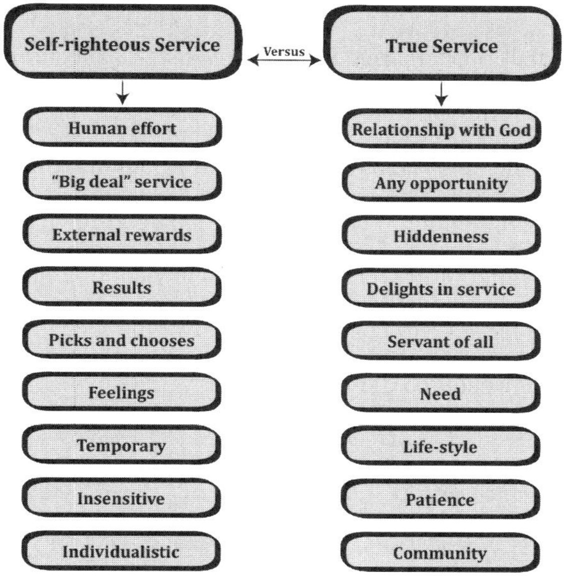

22 Foster. P. 128-130.

remain true service. If you are not serving, think of an area you have served in before, or could serve in the future.

Service is also a spiritual discipline that can, and must be fostered and practiced – "It is not a code of ethics, but a way of living."[23] Here are some practical ways you can start to serve your church, your city, and the nations.

SERVE IN HIDDENESS AND IN THE SMALL THINGS

Throughout Matthew chapter 6, Jesus stresses the importance of hiddenness as we give (v.1, 3-4), pray (v.6), and fast (v.18). Each instruction is followed by a warning of consequence – "they have received their reward" – and a promise – "And your Father who sees in secret will reward you." Jesus concludes the section in versus 19-21 saying,

> *Do not lay up for yourselves treasures on earth, where moth and rust destroy and where thieves break in and steal, but lay up for yourselves treasures in heaven, where neither moth nor rust destroys and where thieves do not break in and steal. For where your treasure is, there your heart will be also.*

---

23 Ibid. P. 134.

In hiddenness, we make God and eternity our focus over our earthly and temporary selves.

"Large tasks require great sacrifice for a moment; small things require constant sacrifice."[24] Thinking about the life of Jesus, it is easy to focus on His death on the cross for our sins as His one, great sacrifice. But we would be forgetting that Jesus' entire life on earth was a huge sacrifice broken up into tiny bits. We often forget that for big things to come together, it is the details – the little things – that matter.

Look for something small that you can do in hiddenness for the people around you and your church. Discuss what some of them might be. Remember that many things are hidden in plain sight!

SERVE IN GUARDING THE REPUTATION OF OTHERS

In a time when entire careers and industries can be forged on simply talking and sharing information about other people, "guarding the reputation of others is a deep and lasting service."[25] James 3:1-12 clearly outlines the dangers of the tongue. "From the same mouth come blessing and cursing." Refusing to take part in gossip is a

24 Ibid. P. 135.

25 Ibid. P. 136.

discipline that must be practiced, so that our mouths can be focused more on blessing.

Do not let anyone talk to you about another brother or sister disparagingly. If they have something they need to air out, it should be done to the person directly. This is something that will take a lot of effort for everyone, but is one of the most important small things that will build the body of Christ the most.

SERVE IN BEING COURTEOUS

Titus 3:2-3 tells us "to be gentle, and to show perfect courtesy toward all people. For we ourselves were once foolish, disobedient, led astray, slaves to various passions and pleasures, passing our days in malice and envy, hated by others and hating one another." But how often have we lashed out at people slamming past us on the street, cutting in front of us in a line or on the road – calling them names and letting our anger run away from us?

The purpose of common courtesy is "to acknowledge others and affirm their worth."[26] Courtesy should not be a reciprocation of how I am treated first. It is part of loving our neighbor – especially in the

26 Ibid. P. 137.

busy urban jungle we live in.

SERVE IN LISTENING

It has commonly been said that, "People don't care how much you know until they know how much you care." The simple act of listening shows that you care about them, that what they say matters to you. This requires compassion and patience.

When people talk more than they listen, it is usually not so much that they lack compassion, but are filled with the need for self-justification. Talking is a great self-justifier. We want to be known, to be appreciated, and for people to think of us as we want them to – so we make sure we get our point across. But as we learn to listen, one of the "fruits… is the freedom to let God be our justifier."[27] Our worth is set by God as our creator and we can trust that nothing can change that.

There is a time to talk, and a time to listen. During your conversations and discussions, be mindful to give everyone plenty of time to do both.

---

27 Ibic. P. 101.

TAKE AWAY: HEAD – HEART – HANDS

Thinking back on the chapter on Service and Ministry, would you agree with the statement that, "You're not really part of a church until you're serving the church."? What ramifications does your answer have for your place in your church right now?

Have you been serving in your church in the past 3 months? If not, what has been stopping you? After this chapter, what will you do?

If you have been serving in your church in the past 3 months, share some of the:

- Joys
- Areas of growth

- Difficulties
- How fulfilled you feel in your current ministry(s) and how effective you feel you are.

INTERCESSION

FOR YOURSELF

Pray for a better understanding and appreciation of how God created you. The key to living the life we are meant to live is to look to God, not within ourselves. Take some time this week to kneel before the Lord in surrender, seeking intimacy with Him with everything you have. Ask Him for His passion and His heart.

FOR THE CHURCH

Pray over specific needs that have either been announced or that you are aware of in your church such as fundraising needs, ministry volunteer needs, or any other types of needs that your church has. If you don't know, find out. Pray for the needs of your church earnestly, Be sensitive to God's leading as he may be guiding you towards meeting some of those needs.

FOR THE CITY

Pray over the needs of people in your city – focus on those your church intentionally serves right now. Pray that people from your church would step up and serve and love the city. See how God may want to use you and your gifts and passions to bless the city.

FOR THE NATIONS

Pray that your church and the church world wide would use its gifts to bless the nations. See if there is a uinque way your church can support missions. Many churches have traditional missions, but there may be a group of people in your church that can bless a missionary, church or organization in a unique and special way.

MEMORY VERSE

Who, though he was in the form of God, did not count equality with God a thing to be grasped, but made himself nothing, taking the form of a servant, being born in the likeness of men. –Philippians 2:6-7

OUTREACH: FINISHING THE MISSION

Let the peoples praise you, O God;

let all the peoples praise you!

Let the nations be glad and sing for joy,

for you judge the peoples with equity

and guide the nations upon earth. Selah

Let the peoples praise you, O God;

let all the peoples praise you!

-Psalm 67:3-5

"He is no fool who gives what he cannot keep to gain that which he cannot lose." - Jim Elliot

INTERACTION

If you only had 5 minutes to spend with loved ones before you died, what would you say to them?

____

____

Last words are pretty important, especially to those that we love. What were the last words of Jesus before He went up into heaven? (Matthew 28:18-20). How much of a priority should those words have on His disciples?

INTRODUCTION

As John Piper says, "Missions exists because worship doesn't." We do missions so that the people might know the glory of God. Outreach comes in many forms. In the most basic form, it is reaching out to others in need of the gospel of Jesus Christ. It is finding ways to share the eternal life-giving message that Jesus saves.

A BASIC PLAN FOR OUTREACH

EVANGELISM

The first form of outreach within our lives would involve sharing our faith and a verbal gospel witness through evangelism. Evangelism is simply telling someone the good news that Jesus Christ came to die for our sins and to give us eternal life with Him for all who trust in Him.

Read Romans 1:16 and Acts 20:24 and write down the things that strike you about Paul's view of sharing the gospel of Jesus Christ.

____

____

Review the earlier chapters on the gospel and read Romans 6:23. How would you share the basics of the gospel to someone who doesn't know?

____

____

Another way we can share the gospel is through telling people our story of how we came to faith in Christ (which is also called our testimony). A testimony would usually have three basic parts to it:

1. What was my life like before knowing Jesus? What needs,

fears, or struggles did I have that make me realize I was in need of a savior? In particular, how did I recognize I was a sinner in need of a savior?

2. How did I come to put my faith and trust in Jesus.
3. What is the difference Christ has made in my life? How have I changed?

Think of sharing your testimony simply as a way of boasting and bragging about the great work Christ has done in your life.

Take some time to write out your testimony and share it with someone today.

MERCY, COMPASSION, AND JUSTICE

While our verbal witness is primary in terms of sharing the gospel, it is not the only way we share the message and love of Jesus. We must not only be a verbal witness for Jesus, we must also be a visible witness and express the gospel through love, mercy, and justice. It is another way of loving our neighbors as ourselves.

Read the following verses and write down what they reveal about the place of justice in God's kingdom?

Psalm 89:14

____

____

Isaiah 1:17

____

____

Psalm 82:3-4

____

____

James 1:27

____

____

What do these verses reveal about God's heart for the vulnerable and oppressed?

____

____

MISSIONS

What does Acts 1:8 and Genesis 12:1-3 reveal about the spread of the gospel?

____

____

____

Ultimately, finishing the mission of Jesus is about local and global evangelization as we love our neighbors through declaring and demonstrating the gospel of Jesus Christ. While we are called to do outreach within our local communities and neighborhoods, it must not stop there. The great commission Jesus gave was a call to go to the ends of the earth, and that's where our focus will go next.

INSTRUCTION

THE PRIORITY OF MISSIONS

What will it take to finish the mission that Jesus gave us to do?

A PEOPLE COMMITTED TO INTIMACY

This is probably not the first thing you would've expected to read on a chapter concerning missions work, but it's foundational. In fact, intimacy with God is the foundation of missions work and the fuel that will keep the missions flame burning in our hearts.

Read Matthew 22:37-40. How would these verses be connected to missions?

____

____

____

The greatest thing we can do in life is to love God with everything that we have. After that, the greatest thing is to love others as ourselves. Everything God desires from His people is an overflow of these two commandments. The great commandment is the only way for the great commission to be possible. Because before we are called to go, we are called to come. Jesus says, "Come to me" (Matthew 11:28) and that is our calling from Him everyday.

What did Jesus appoint the twelve apostles to do in Mark 3:14?

____

____

____

What does 1 Thessalonians 5:9-10 say is one of the reasons for our salvation?

____

____

These verses and others throughout Scripture show how much God wants to simply be with us because He loves us. Throughout the Psalms, it declares "how great is His love!" As we deepen our love relationship with Jesus, we realize that His love becomes our song and His love becomes our strength.

Love must be the highest motive of service if we're going to last on the mission field and especially last through seasons of suffering. Our ultimate motive for missions is not because of need, nor guilt. Our motive is because we love Jesus so much and want others to know Him. And because we love Jesus so much and He loves the nations so much, our desire is to give Him what He desires. That is the only way the mission can be completed.

A PEOPLE COMMITTED TO INTERCESSION

Another thing that is needed if we're going to finish the mission

Jesus gave us to do is to be a people committed to prayer and intercession for the lost. True love leads to prayer. True love for God leads us to pray to God. True love for others leads us to pray for others. True love leads to prayer. And intercession is where the love for God and love for others meet together.

Read Matthew 9:35-38 and write down what Jesus was doing, how Jesus was feeling, and what Jesus asks His disciples to do.

____

____

What's the connection between prayer and missions?

____

____

What's something we can learn to pray for concerning the work of missions that we find in 2 Thessalonians 3:1?

____

____

A couple of resources to help you pray for missions is to use the book Operation World by Jason Mandryk (www.operationworld.org)

and the prayer guide Global Prayer Digest (www.globalprayerdigest.org). Operation World is an excellent book that gives you prayer guides and key stats on every country in the world. Praying through this book will allow you to intercede for all the nations of the world. And Global Prayer Digest is a daily prayer guide published monthly that will help you pray through a different unreached people group each day. According to the Lausanne Movement, an unreached people group refers to a unique ethnic group without an indigenous, self-propagating Christian church movement. Any ethnic or ethnolinguistic nation without enough Christians to evangelize the rest of the nation would be considered an unreached people group. They would usually have no Christians or very few Christians within their reach or within their culture or communities, therefore they should be a high priority for the Church in terms of prayer and missions strategy (which we'll get to more in a moment).

Find out who the supported missionaries in your church are and write their names here and begin to pray for them on a regular basis.

____

____

A PEOPLE COMMITTED TO INFILTRATION

Another way that we will finish the mission of Jesus is to have a people committed to infiltration. This is a war term of strategically attacking and dismantling areas once ruled by the enemy and overthrowing its power. We need to use a war term because the fight we are in is war. But this battle is not against other people, not against flesh and blood, but against the power of darkness that blinds and deceives the hearts of people from knowing Jesus.

What does Matthew 24:14 tell us about what will happen before the end comes?

____

____

In light of this, why should missions be a high priority for the Church?

____

____

Two “windows” you need to be familiar with are the 10/40 Window and the 4/14 Window.

The 10/40 Window refers to the geographical part of the world 10 degrees north of the equator to 40 degrees north of the equator spanning from Africa to Asia. 84% of all unreached people groups

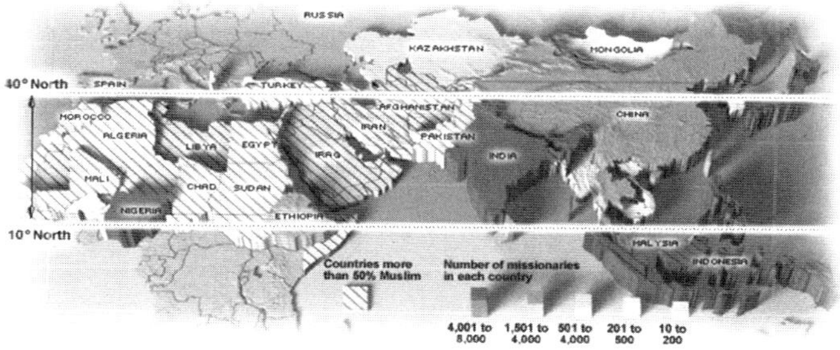

live within the 10/40 window. This is also where the largest number of Muslims, Hindus, and Buddhists live. As a result, this region of the world should also have a high priority in terms of our missions praying, giving, sending, and going.

The other window you should be familiar with connected to missions is the 4/14 window. This window doesn't have to do with geography, it has to do with the range of children between the ages of 4 and 14. Studies have found that children are most receptive to understand and receive the gospel message within this window of ages. So this too should play a vital role in our missions strategy.

How should the 10/40 and 4/14 Windows impact your life? What should it change about how we live, pray, give, and do ministry?

TAKE AWAY: HEAD – HEART – HANDS

What was something that challenged you this chapter on outreach? How will you pray differently now? How will you give differently now? How can you also get on mission with God in order to help finish His mission?

INTERCESSION

FOR YOURSELF

Make a list and pray for the people in your life that need to know the love of Jesus, and look for opportunities to share the gospel with them. Pray that you will be a light in your community and share the gospel in your city on a regular basis.

FOR THE CHURCH

Pray through the list of missionaries that your church supports and faithfully cover them with prayers. Pray also that God will give more people in your church a heart for the lost and that more people will be send out by the church to different countries that need Jesus.

FOR THE CITY

Pray prayers of repentance on behalf of the sins of your city. Ask the Lord for mercy and revival for your community. Pray that the churches in your city would remain faithful to preaching the cross of Christ and be used by God to spread the gospel effectively.

FOR THE NATIONS

Begin making a list of people groups and countries to pray for on a regular basis (you can visit www.joshuaproject.net for a comprehensive list of unreached people groups). Pray for the churches in other nations to grow and be strong in their witness for the Lord. And finally pray that all the nations of the earth would filled with the gospel and the glory of the Lord.

CONCLUSION

Congratulations on completing the first part of this book! What's the next part? Teaching someone else what you just learned. Our goal is not just to learn, but to teach. Because to be a disciple means we are continually making disciples of others. So may you love your neighbors by pointing them to Jesus, and may you take what you've learned throughout this book and teach these precious truths to others.

Go therefore and make disciples of all nations, baptizing them in the name of the Father and of the Son and of the Holy Spirit, [20] teaching them to observe all that I have commanded you. And behold, I am with you always, to the end of the age."

- Matthew 28:19-20

Who will you disciple next? Let's go. Let's make disciples. And let's finish the mission.

APPENDIX 1
BIBLE IN ONE YEAR

MCCHEYNE BIBLE READING PLAN

M'Cheyne Bible Reading Plan (www.esv.org/biblereadingplans)

Jan 1 Gen 1, Matt 1, Ezra 1, Acts 1

Jan 2 Gen 2, Matt 2, Ezra 2, Acts 2

Jan 3 Gen 3, Matt 3, Ezra 3, Acts 3

Jan 4 Gen 4, Matt 4, Ezra 4, Acts 4

Jan 5 Gen 5, Matt 5, Ezra 5, Acts 5

Jan 6 Gen 6, Matt 6, Ezra 6, Acts 6

Jan 7 Gen 7, Matt 7, Ezra 7, Acts 7

Jan 8 Gen 8, Matt 8, Ezra 8, Acts 8

Jan 9 Gen 9-10, Matt 9, Ezra 9, Acts 9

Jan 10 Gen 11, Matt 10, Ezra 10, Acts 10

Jan 11 Gen 12, Matt 11, Neh 1, Acts 11

Jan 12 Gen 13, Matt 12, Neh 2, Acts 12

Jan 13 Gen 14, Matt 13, Neh 3, Acts 13

Jan 14 Gen 15, Matt 14, Neh 4, Acts 14

Jan 15 Gen 16, Matt 15, Neh 5, Acts 15

Jan 16 Gen 17, Matt 16, Neh 6, Acts 16

Jan 17 Gen 18, Matt 17, Neh 7, Acts 17

Jan 18 Gen 19, Matt 18, Neh 8, Acts 18

Jan 19 Gen 20, Matt 19, Neh 9, Acts 19

Jan 20 Gen 21, Matt 20, Neh 10, Acts 20

Jan 21 Gen 22, Matt 21, Neh 11, Acts 21

Jan 22 Gen 23, Matt 22, Neh 12, Acts 22

Jan 23 Gen 24, Matt 23, Neh 13, Acts 23

Jan 24 Gen 25, Matt 24, Est 1, Acts 24

Jan 25 Gen 26, Matt 25, Est 2, Acts 25

Jan 26 Gen 27, Matt 26, Est 3, Acts 26

Jan 27 Gen 28, Matt 27, Est 4, Acts 27

Jan 28 Gen 29, Matt 28, Est 5, Acts 28

Jan 29 Gen 30, Mark 1, Est 6, Rom 1

Jan 30 Gen 31, Mark 2, Est 7, Rom 2

Jan 31 Gen 32, Mark 3, Est 8, Rom 3

Feb 1 Gen 33, Mark 4, Est 9-10, Rom 4

Feb 2 Gen 34, Mark 5, Job 1, Rom 5

Feb 3 Gen 35-36, Mark 6, Job 2, Rom 6

Feb 4 Gen 37, Mark 7, Job 3, Rom 7

Feb 5 Gen 38, Mark 8, Job 4, Rom 8

Feb 6 Gen 39, Mark 9, Job 5, Rom 9

Feb 7 Gen 40, Mark 10, Job 6, Rom 10

Feb 8 Gen 41, Mark 11, Job 7, Rom 11

Feb 9 Gen 42, Mark 12, Job 8, Rom 12

Feb 10 Gen 43, Mark 13, Job 9, Rom 13

Feb 11 Gen 44, Mark 14, Job 10, Rom 14

Feb 12 Gen 45, Mark 15, Job 11, Rom 15

Feb 13 Gen 46, Mark 16, Job 12, Rom 16

Feb 14 Gen 47, Luke 1:1-38, Job 13, 1 Cor 1

Feb 15 Gen 48, Luke 1:39-80, Job 14, 1 Cor 2

Feb 16 Gen 49, Luke 2, Job 15, 1 Cor 3

Feb 17 Gen 50, Luke 3, Job 16-17, 1 Cor 4

Feb 18 Ex 1, Luke 4, Job 18, 1 Cor 5

Feb 19 Ex 2, Luke 5, Job 19, 1 Cor 6

Feb 20 Ex 3, Luke 6, Job 20, 1 Cor 7

Feb 21 Ex 4, Luke 7, Job 21, 1 Cor 8

Feb 22 Ex 5, Luke 8, Job 22, 1 Cor 9

Feb 23 Ex 6, Luke 9, Job 23, 1 Cor 10

Feb 24 Ex 7, Luke 10, Job 24, 1 Cor 11

Feb 25 Ex 8, Luke 11, Job 25-26, 1 Cor 12

Feb 26 Ex 9, Luke 12, Job 27, 1 Cor 13

Feb 27 Ex 10, Luke 13, Job 28, 1 Cor 14

Feb 28 Ex 11, Luke 14, Job 29, 1 Cor 15

Mar 1 Ex 12, Luke 15, Job 30, 1 Cor 16

Mar 2 Ex 13, Luke 16, Job 31, 2 Cor 1

Mar 3 Ex 14, Luke 17, Job 32, 2 Cor 2

Mar 4 Ex 15, Luke 18, Job 33, 2 Cor 3

Mar 5 Ex 16, Luke 19, Job 34, 2 Cor 4

Mar 6 Ex 17, Luke 20, Job 35, 2 Cor 5

Mar 7 Ex 18, Luke 21, Job 36, 2 Cor 6

Mar 8 Ex 19, Luke 22, Job 37, 2 Cor 7

Mar 9 Ex 20, Luke 23, Job 38, 2 Cor 8

Mar 10 Ex 21, Luke 24, Job 39, 2 Cor 9

Mar 11 Ex 22, John 1, Job 40, 2 Cor 10

Mar 12 Ex 23, John 2, Job 41, 2 Cor 11

Mar 13 Ex 24, John 3, Job 42, 2 Cor 12

Mar 14 Ex 25, John 4, Prov 1, 2 Cor 13

Mar 15 Ex 26, John 5, Prov 2, Gal 1

Mar 16 Ex 27, John 6, Prov 3, Gal 2

Mar 17 Ex 28, John 7, Prov 4, Gal 3

Mar 18 Ex 29, John 8, Prov 5, Gal 4

Mar 19 Ex 30, John 9, Prov 6, Gal 5

Mar 20 Ex 31, John 10, Prov 7, Gal 6

Mar 21 Ex 32, John 11, Prov 8, Eph 1

Mar 22 Ex 33, John 12, Prov 9, Eph 2

Mar 23 Ex 34, John 13, Prov 10, Eph 3

Mar 24 Ex 35, John 14, Prov 11, Eph 4

Mar 25 Ex 36, John 15, Prov 12, Eph 5

Mar 26 Ex 37, John 16, Prov 13, Eph 6

Mar 27 Ex 38, John 17, Prov 14, Phil 1

Mar 28 Ex 39, John 18, Prov 15, Phil 2

Mar 29 Ex 40, John 19, Prov 16, Phil 3

Mar 30 Lev 1, John 20, Prov 17, Phil 4

Mar 31 Lev 2-3, John 21, Prov 18, Col 1

Apr 1 Lev 4, Ps 1-2, Prov 19, Col 2

Apr 2 Lev 5, Ps 3-4, Prov 20, Col 3

Apr 3 Lev 6, Ps 5-6, Prov 21, Col 4

Apr 4 Lev 7, Ps 7-8, Prov 22, 1 Thes 1

Apr 5 Lev 8, Ps 9, Prov 23, 1 Thes 2

Apr 6 Lev 9, Ps 10, Prov 24, 1 Thes 3

Apr 7 Lev 10, Ps 11-12, Prov 25, 1 Thes 4

Apr 8 Lev 11-12, Ps 13-14, Prov 26, 1 Thes 5

Apr 9 Lev 13, Ps 15-16, Prov 27, 2 Thes 1

Apr 10 Lev 14, Ps 17, Prov 28, 2 Thes 2

Apr 11 Lev 15, Ps 18, Prov 29, 2 Thes 3

Apr 12 Lev 16, Ps 19, Prov 30, 1 Tim 1

Apr 13 Lev 17, Ps 20-21, Prov 31, 1 Tim 2

Apr 14 Lev 18, Ps 22, Eccl 1, 1 Tim 3

Apr 15 Lev 19, Ps 23-24, Eccl 2, 1 Tim 4

Apr 16 Lev 20, Ps 25, Eccl 3, 1 Tim 5

Apr 17 Lev 21, Ps 26-27, Eccl 4, 1 Tim 6

Apr 18 Lev 22, Ps 28-29, Eccl 5, 2 Tim 1

Apr 19 Lev 23, Ps 30, Eccl 6, 2 Tim 2

Apr 20 Lev 24, Ps 31, Eccl 7, 2 Tim 3

Apr 21 Lev 25, Ps 32, Eccl 8, 2 Tim 4

Apr 22 Lev 26, Ps 33, Eccl 9, Titus 1

Apr 23 Lev 27, Ps 34, Eccl 10, Titus 2

Apr 24 Num 1, Ps 35, Eccl 11, Titus 3

Apr 25 Num 2, Ps 36, Eccl 12, Phm 1

Apr 26 Num 3, Ps 37, Sng 1, Heb 1

Apr 27 Num 4, Ps 38, Sng 2, Heb 2

Apr 28 Num 5, Ps 39, Sng 3, Heb 3

Apr 29 Num 6, Ps 40-41, Sng 4, Heb 4

Apr 30 Num 7, Ps 42-43, Sng 5, Heb 5

May 1 Num 8, Ps 44, Sng 6, Heb 6

May 2 Num 9, Ps 45, Sng 7, Heb 7

May 3 Num 10, Ps 46-47, Sng 8, Heb 8

May 4 Num 11, Ps 48, Isa 1, Heb 9

May 5 Num 12-13, Ps 49, Isa 2, Heb 10

May 6 Num 14, Ps 50, Isa 3-4, Heb 11

May 7 Num 15, Ps 51, Isa 5, Heb 12

May 8 Num 16, Ps 52-54, Isa 6, Heb 13

May 9 Num 17-18, Ps 55, Isa 7, Jas 1

May 10 Num 19, Ps 56-57, Isa 8, Jas 2

May 11 Num 20, Ps 58-59, Isa 9, Jas 3

May 12 Num 21, Ps 60-61, Isa 10, Jas 4

May 13 Num 22, Ps 62-63, Isa 11-12, Jas 5

May 14 Num 23, Ps 64-65, Isa 13, 1 Pet 1

May 15 Num 24, Ps 66-67, Isa 14, 1 Pet 2

May 16 Num 25, Ps 68, Isa 15, 1 Pet 3

May 17 Num 26, Ps 69, Isa 16, 1 Pet 4

May 18 Num 27, Ps 70-71, Isa 17-18, 1 Pet 5

May 19 Num 28, Ps 72, Isa 19-20, 2 Pet 1

May 20 Num 29, Ps 73, Isa 21, 2 Pet 2

May 21 Num 30, Ps 74, Isa 22, 2 Pet 3

May 22 Num 31, Ps 75-76, Isa 23, 1 Jn 1

May 23 Num 32, Ps 77, Isa 24, 1 Jn 2

May 24 Num 33, Ps 78:1-39, Isa 25, 1 Jn 3

May 25 Num 34, Ps 78:40-72, Isa 26, 1 Jn 4

May 26 Num 35, Ps 79, Isa 27, 1 Jn 5

May 27 Num 36, Ps 80, Isa 28, 2 Jn 1

May 28 Deut 1, Ps 81-82, Isa 29, 3 Jn 1

May 29 Deut 2, Ps 83-84, Isa 30, Jude 1

May 30 Deut 3, Ps 85, Isa 31, Rev 1

May 31 Deut 4, Ps 86-87, Isa 32, Rev 2

Jun 1 Deut 5, Ps 88, Isa 33, Rev 3

Jun 2 Deut 6, Ps 89, Isa 34, Rev 4

Jun 3 Deut 7, Ps 90, Isa 35, Rev 5

Jun 4 Deut 8, Ps 91, Isa 36, Rev 6

Jun 5 Deut 9, Ps 92-93, Isa 37, Rev 7

Jun 6 Deut 10, Ps 94, Isa 38, Rev 8

Jun 7 Deut 11, Ps 95-96, Isa 39, Rev 9

Jun 8 Deut 12, Ps 97-98, Isa 40,Rev 10

Jun 9 Deut 13-14, Ps 99-101, Isa 41, Rev 11

Jun 10 Deut 15, Ps 102, Isa 42, Rev 12

Jun 11 Deut 16, Ps 103, Isa 43, Rev 13

Jun 12 Deut 17, Ps 104, Isa 44, Rev 14

Jun 13 Deut 18, Ps 105, Isa 45, Rev 15

Jun 14 Deut 19, Ps 106, Isa 46, Rev 16

Jun 15 Deut 20, Ps 107, Isa 47, Rev 17

Jun 16 Deut 21, Ps 108-109, Isa 48, Rev 18

Jun 17 Deut 22, Ps 110-111, Isa 49, Rev 19

Jun 18 Deut 23, Ps 112-113, Isa 50,Rev 20

Jun 19 Deut 24, Ps 114-115, Isa 51, Rev 21

Jun 20 Deut 25, Ps 116, Isa 52, Rev 22

Jun 21 Deut 26, Ps 117-118, Isa 53, Matt 1

Jun 22 Deut 27, Ps 119:1-24, Isa 54, Matt 2

Jun 23 Deut 28,Ps 119:25-48, Isa 55, Matt 3

Jun 24 Deut 29, Ps 119:49-72, Isa 56, Matt 4

Jun 25 Deut 30, Ps 119:73-96, Isa 57, Matt 5

Jun 26 Deut 31, Ps 119:97-120, Isa 58, Matt 6

Jun 27 Deut 32, Ps 119:121-144, Isa 59, Matt 7

Jun 28 Deut 33-34, Ps 119:145-176, Isa 60, Matt 8

Jun 29 Josh 1, Ps 120-122, Isa 61, Matt 9

Jun 30 Josh 2, Ps 123-125, Isa 62, Matt 10

Jul 1 Josh 3, Ps 126-128, Isa 63, Matt 11

Jul 2 Josh 4,Ps 129-131, Isa 64, Matt 12

Jul 3 Josh 5, Ps 132-134, Isa 65, Matt 13

Jul 4 Josh 6, Ps 135-136, Isa 66, Matt 14

Jul 5 Josh 7, Ps 137-138, Jer 1, Matt 15

Jul 6 Josh 8, Ps 139, Jer 2, Matt 16

Jul 7 Josh 9, Ps 140-141, Jer 3, Matt 17

Jul 8 Josh 10, Ps 142-143, Jer 4, Matt 18

Jul 9 Josh 11, Ps 144, Jer 5, Matt 19

Jul 10 Josh 12-13, Ps 145, Jer 6, Matt 20

Jul 11 Josh 14-15, Ps 146-147, Jer 7, Matt 21

Jul 12 Josh 16-17, Ps 148, Jer 8, Matt 22

Jul 13 Josh 18-19, Ps 149-150, Jer 9, Matt 23

Jul 14 Josh 20-21, Acts 1, Jer 10,

Jul 15 Josh 22, Acts 2, Jer 11, Matt 25

Jul 16 Josh 23, Acts 3, Jer 12, Matt 26

Jul 17 Josh 24, Acts 4, Jer 13, Matt 27

Jul 18 Judg 1, Acts 5, Jer 14, Matt 28

Jul 19 Judg 2, Acts 6, Jer 15, Mark 1

Jul 20 Judg 3, Acts 7, Jer 16, Mark 2

Jul 21 Judg 4, Acts 8, Jer 17, Mark 3

Jul 22 Judg 5, Acts 9, Jer 18, Mark 4

Jul 23 Judg 6, Acts 10, Jer 19, Mark 5

Jul 24 Judg 7, Acts 11, Jer 20, Mark 6

Jul 25 Judg 8, Acts 12, Jer 21, Mark 7

Jul 26 Judg 9, Acts 13, Jer 22, Mark 8

Jul 27 Judg 10, Acts 14, Jer 23, Mark 9

Jul 28 Judg 11, Acts 15, Jer 24, Mark 10

Jul 29 Judg 12, Acts 16, Jer 25, Mark 11

Jul 30 Judg 13, Acts 17, Jer 26, Mark 12

Jul 31 Judg 14, Acts 18, Jer 27, Mark 13

Aug 1 Judg 15, Acts 19, Jer 28, Mark 14

Aug 2 Judg 16, Acts 20, Jer 29, Mark 15

Aug 3 Judg 17, Acts 21, Jer 30-31, Mark 16

Aug 4 Judg 18, Acts 22, Jer 32, Luke 1

Aug 5 Judg 19, Acts 23, Jer 33, Luke 2

Aug 6 Judg 20, Acts 24, Jer 34, Luke 3

Aug 7 Judg 21, Acts 25, Jer 35, Luke 4

Aug 8 Ruth 1, Acts 26, Jer 36, Luke 5

Aug 9 Ruth 2, Acts 27, Jer 37, Luke 6

Aug 10 Ruth 3-4, Acts 28, Jer 38, Luke 7

Aug 11 1 Sam 1, Rom 1, Jer 39, Luke 8

Aug 12 1 Sam 2, Rom 2, Jer 40, Luke 9

Aug 13 1 Sam 3, Rom 3, Jer 41, Luke 10

Aug 14 1 Sam 4, Rom 4, Jer 42, Luke 11

Aug 15 1 Sam 5-6, Rom 5, Jer 43, Luke 12

Aug 16 1 Sam 7-8, Rom 6, Jer 44-45, Luke 13

Aug 17 1 Sam 9, Rom 7, Jer 46, Luke 14

Aug 18 1 Sam 10, Rom 8, Jer 47, Luke 15

Aug 19 1 Sam 11, Rom 9, Jer 48, Luke 16

Aug 20 1 Sam 12, Rom 10, Jer 49, Luke 17

Aug 21 1 Sam 13, Rom 11, Jer 50, Luke 18

Aug 22 1 Sam 14, Rom 12, Jer 51, Luke 19

Aug 23 1 Sam 15, Rom 13, Jer 52, Luke 20

Aug 24 1 Sam 16, Rom 14, Lam 1, Luke 21

Aug 25 1 Sam 17, Rom 15, Lam 2, Luke 22

Aug 26 1 Sam 18, Rom 16, Lam 3, Luke 23

Aug 27 1 Sam 19, 1 Cor 1, Lam 4, Luke 24

Aug 28 1 Sam 20, 1 Cor 2, Lam 5, John 1

Aug 29 1 Sam 21-22, 1 Cor 3, Ezek 1, John 2

Aug 30 1 Sam 23, 1 Cor 4, Ezek 2, John 3

Aug 31 1 Sam 24, 1 Cor 5, Ezek 3, John 4

Sep 1 1 Sam 25, 1 Cor 6, Ezek 4, John 5

Sep 2 1 Sam 26, 1 Cor 7, Ezek 5, John 6

Sep 3 1 Sam 27, 1 Cor 8, Ezek 6, John 7

Sep 4 1 Sam 28, 1 Cor 9, Ezek 7, John 8

Sep 5 1 Sam 29-30, 1 Cor 10, Ezek 8, John 9

Sep 6 1 Sam 31, 1 Cor 11, Ezek 9, John 10

Sep 7 2 Sam 1, 1 Cor 12, Ezek 10, John 11

Sep 8 2 Sam 2, 1 Cor 13, Ezek 11, John 12

Sep 9 2 Sam 3, 1 Cor 14, Ezek 12, John 13

Sep 10 2 Sam 4-5, 1 Cor 15, Ezek 13, John 14

Sep 11 2 Sam 6, 1 Cor 16, Ezek 14, John 15

Sep 12 2 Sam 7, 2 Cor 1, Ezek 15, John 16

Sep 13 2 Sam 8-9, 2 Cor 2, Ezek 16, John 17

Sep 14 2 Sam 10, 2 Cor 3, Ezek 17, John 18

Sep 15 2 Sam 11, 2 Cor 4, Ezek 18, John 19

Sep 16 2 Sam 12, 2 Cor 5, Ezek 19, John 20

Sep 17 2 Sam 13, 2 Cor 6, Ezek 20, John 21

Sep 18 2 Sam 14, 2 Cor 7, Ezek 21, Ps 1-2

Sep 19 2 Sam 15, 2 Cor 8, Ezek 22, Ps 3-4

Sep 20 2 Sam 16, 2 Cor 9, Ezek 23, Ps 5-6

Sep 21 2 Sam 17, 2 Cor 10, Ezek 24, Ps 7-8

Sep 22 2 Sam 18, 2 Cor 11, Ezek 25, Ps 9

Sep 23 2 Sam 19, 2 Cor 12, Ezek 26, Ps 10

Sep 24 2 Sam 20, 2 Cor 13, Ezek 27, Ps 11-12

Sep 25 2 Sam 21, Gal 1, Ezek 28, Ps 13-14

Sep 26 2 Sam 22, Gal 2, Ezek 29, Ps 15-16

Sep 27 2 Sam 23, Gal 3, Ezek 30, Ps 17

Sep 28 2 Sam 24, Gal 4, Ezek 31, Ps 18

Sep 29 1 Kgs 1, Gal 5, Ezek 32, Ps 19

Sep 30 1 Kgs 2, Gal 6, Ezek 33, Ps 20-21

Oct 1 1 Kgs 3, Eph 1, Ezek 34, Ps 22

Oct 2 1 Kgs 4-5, Eph 2, Ezek 35, Ps 23-24

Oct 3 1 Kgs 6, Eph 3, Ezek 36, Ps 25

Oct 4 1 Kgs 7, Eph 4, Ezek 37, Ps 26-27

Oct 5 1 Kgs 8, Eph 5, Ezek 38,Ps 28-29

Oct 6 1 Kgs 9, Eph 6, Ezek 39, Ps 30

Oct 7 1 Kgs 10, Phil 1, Ezek 40, Ps 31

Oct 8 1 Kgs 11, Phil 2, Ezek 41, Ps 32

Oct 9 1 Kgs 12, Phil 3, Ezek 42, Ps 33

Oct 10 1 Kgs 13, Phil 4, Ezek 43, Ps 34

Oct 11 1 Kgs 14, Col 1, Ezek 44, Ps 35

Oct 12 1 Kgs 15, Col 2, Ezek 45, Ps 36

Oct 13 1 Kgs 16, Col 3, Ezek 46, Ps 37

Oct 14 1 Kgs 17, Col 4, Ezek 47, Ps 38

Oct 15 1 Kgs 18, 1 Thes 1, Ezek 48, Ps 39

Oct 16 1 Kgs 19, 1 Thes 2, Dan 1, Ps 40-41

Oct 17 1 Kgs 20, 1 Thes 3, Dan 2, Ps 42-43

Oct 18 1 Kgs 21, 1 Thes 4, Dan 3, Ps 44

Oct 19 1 Kgs 22, 1 Thes 5, Dan 4, Ps 45

Oct 20 2 Kgs 1, 2 Thes 1, Dan 5, Ps 46-47

Oct 21 2 Kgs 2, 2 Thes 2, Dan 6, Ps 48

Oct 22 2 Kgs 3, 2 Thes 3, Dan 7, Ps 49

Oct 23 2 Kgs 4, 1 Tim 1, Dan 8, Ps 50

Oct 24 2 Kgs 5, 1 Tim 2, Dan 9, Ps 51

Oct 25 2 Kgs 6, 1 Tim 3, Dan 10, Ps 52-54

Oct 26 2 Kgs 7, 1 Tim 4, Dan 11, Ps 55

Oct 27 2 Kgs 8, 1 Tim 5, Dan 12, Ps 56-57

Oct 28 2 Kgs 9, 1 Tim 6, Hos 1, Ps 58-59

Oct 29 2 Kgs 10-11, 2 Tim 1, Hos 2, Ps 60-61

Oct 30 2 Kgs 12, 2 Tim 2, Hos 3-4, Ps 62-63

Oct 31 2 Kgs 13, 2 Tim 3, Hos 5-6, Ps 64-65

Nov 1 2 Kgs 14, 2 Tim 4, Hos 7, Ps 66-67

Nov 2 2 Kgs 15, Titus 1, Hos 8, Ps 68

Nov 3 2 Kgs 16, Titus 2, Hos 9, Ps 69

Nov 4 2 Kgs 17, Titus 3, Hos 10, Ps 70-71

Nov 5 2 Kgs 18, Phm 1, Hos 11, Ps 72

Nov 6 2 Kgs 19, Heb 1, Hos 12, Ps 73

Nov 7 2 Kgs 20, Heb 2, Hos 13, Ps 74

Nov 8 2 Kgs 21, Heb 3, Hos 14, Ps 75-76

Nov 9 2 Kgs 22, Heb 4, Joel 1, Ps 77

Nov 10 2 Kgs 23, Heb 5, Joel 2, Ps 78

Nov 11 2 Kgs 24, Heb 6, Joel 3, Ps 79

Nov 12 2 Kgs 25, Heb 7, Amos 1, Ps 80

Nov 13 1 Chr 1-2, Heb 8, Amos 2, Ps 81-82

Nov 14 1 Chr 3-4, Heb 9, Amos 3, Ps 83-84

Nov 15 1 Chr 5-6, Heb 10, Amos 4, Ps 85

Nov 16 1 Chr 7-8, Heb 11, Amos 5, Ps 86

Nov 17 1 Chr 9-10, Heb 12, Amos 6, Ps 87-88

Nov 18 1 Chr 11-12, Heb 13, Amos 7, Ps 89

Nov 19 1 Chr 13-14, Jas 1, Amos 8, Ps 90

Nov 20 1 Chr 15, Jas 2, Amos 9, Ps 91

Nov 21 1 Chr 16, Jas 3, Obad 1, Ps 92-93

Nov 22 1 Chr 17, Jas 4, Jonah 1, Ps 94

Nov 23 1 Chr 18, Jas 5, Jonah 2, Ps 95-96

Nov 24 1 Chr 19-20, 1 Pet 1, Jonah 3, Ps 97-98

Nov 25 1 Chr 21, 1 Pet 2, Jonah 4, Ps 99-101

Nov 26 1 Chr 22, 1 Pet 3, Mic 1, Ps 102

Nov 27 1 Chr 23, 1 Pet 4, Mic 2, Ps 103

Nov 28 1 Chr 24-25, 1 Pet 5, Mic 3, Ps 104

Nov 29 1 Chr 26-27, 2 Pet 1, Mic 4, Ps 105

Nov 30 1 Chr 28, 2 Pet 2, Mic 5, Ps 106

Dec 1 1 Chr 29, 2 Pet 3, Mic 6, Ps 107

Dec 2 2 Chr 1, 1 Jn 1, Mic 7, Ps 108-109

Dec 3 2 Chr 2, 1 Jn 2, Nahum 1, Ps 110-111

Dec 4 2 Chr 3-4, 1 Jn 3, Nahum 2, Ps 112-113

Dec 5 2 Chr 5, 1 Jn 4, Nahum 3, Ps 114-115

Dec 6 2 Chr 6, 1 Jn 5, Hab 1, Ps 116

Dec 7 2 Chr 7, 2 Jn 1, Hab 2, Ps 117-118

Dec 8 2 Chr 8, 3 Jn 1, Hab 3, Ps 119:1-24

Dec 9 2 Chr 9, Jude 1, Zeph 1, Ps 119:25-48

Dec 10 2 Chr 10, Rev 1, Zeph 2, Ps 119:49-72

Dec 11 2 Chr 11-12, Rev 2, Zeph 3, Ps 119:73-96

Dec 12 2 Chr 13, Rev 3, Hag 1, Ps 119:97-120

Dec 13 2 Chr 14-15, Rev 4, Hag 2, Ps 119:121-144

Dec 14 2 Chr 16, Rev 5, Zech 1,Ps 119:145-176

Dec 15 2 Chr 17, Rev 6, Zech 2, Ps 120-122

Dec 16 2 Chr 18, Rev 7, Zech 3, Ps 123-125

Dec 17 2 Chr 19-20, Rev 8, Zech 4, Ps 126-128

Dec 18 2 Chr 21, Rev 9, Zech 5, Ps 129-131

Dec 19 2 Chr 22-23, Rev 10, Zech 6, Ps 132-134

Dec 20 2 Chr 24, Rev 11, Zech 7, Ps 135-136

Dec 21 2 Chr 25, Rev 12, Zech 8, Ps 137-138

Dec 22 2 Chr 26, Rev 13, Zech 9, Ps 139

Dec 23 2 Chr 27-28, Rev 14, Zech 10, Ps 140-141

Dec 24 2 Chr 29, Rev 15, Zech 11, Ps 142

Dec 25 2 Chr 30, Rev 16, Zech 12, Ps 143

Dec 26 2 Chr 31, Rev 17, Zech 13, Ps 144

Dec 27 2 Chr 32, Rev 18, Zech 14, Ps 145

Dec 28 2 Chr 33, Rev 19, Mal 1, Ps 146-147

Dec 29 2 Chr 34, Rev 20, Mal 2, Ps 148

Dec 30 2 Chr 35, Rev 21, Mal 3, Ps 149

Dec 31 2 Chr 36, Rev 22, Mal 4, Ps 150

APPENDIX 2

ADDITIONAL QUESTIONS FOR ACCOUNTABILITY

The following is an article written by Ed Stetzer in Christianity Today.[30]

Yesterday, I finished up my series through James. I promised to include some accountability question list examples here. These lists are from Cultivating a Life for God (Church Smart Resources 1999 pp.125-131).

Typically, these questions are asked in groups of 2-3, are specific to men or women, meets regularly, and hold each other accountable.

JOHN WESLEY'S SMALL GROUP QUESTIONS

1. Am I consciously or unconsciously creating the impression that I am better than I am? In other words, am I a hypocrite?
2. Am I honest in all my acts and words, or do I exaggerate?
3. Do I confidentially pass onto another what was told me in confidence?

30 http://www.christianitytoday.com/edstetzer/2008/may/accountability-questions.html

4. Am I a slave to dress, friends, work , or habits?

5. Am I self-conscious, self-pitying, or self-justifying?

6. Did the Bible live in me today?

7. Do I give it time to speak to me everyday?

8. Am I enjoying prayer?

9. When did I last speak to someone about my faith?

10. Do I pray about the money I spend?

11. Do I get to bed on time and get up on time?

12. Do I disobey God in anything?

13. Do I insist upon doing something about which my conscience is uneasy?

14. Am I defeated in any part of my life?

15. Am I jealous, impure, critical, irritable, touchy or distrustful?

16. How do I spend my spare time?

17. Am I proud?

18. Do I thank God that I am not as other people, especially as the Pharisee who despised the publican?

19. Is there anyone whom I fear, dislike, disown, criticize, hold resentment toward or disregard? If so, what am I going to do about it?

20. Do I grumble and complain constantly?

21. Is Christ real to me?

WESLEY'S BAND MEETING QUESTIONS:

1. What known sins have you committed since our last meeting?
2. What temptations have you met with?
3. How were you delivered?
4. What have you thought, said, or done, of which you doubt whether it be sin or not?
5. Have you nothing you desire to keep secret?

Reference: John Wesley's Class Meetings: a Model for Making Disciples, by D. Michael Henderson, Evangel Publishing House, 1997, pp. 118-9

CHUCK SWINDOLL'S PASTORAL ACCOUNTABILITY QUESTIONS:

In his book, The Body, Chuck Colson lists the questions used by Chuck Swindoll.

1. Have you been with a woman anywhere this past week that might

be seen as compromising?

2. Have any of your financial dealings lacked integrity?

3. Have you exposed yourself to any sexually explicit material?

4. Have you spent adequate time in Bible study and prayer?

5. Have you given priority time to your family?

6. Have you fulfilled the mandates of your calling?

7. Have you just lied to me?

NEIL COLE

1. What is the condition of your soul?

2. What sin do you need to confess?

3. What have you held back from God that you need to surrender?

4. Is there anything that has dampened your zeal for Christ?

5. Who have you talked with about Christ this week?

HT: Journey

CHURCH MULTIPLICATION ASSOCIATES

The questions I use are from these cards from Church Multiplication Associates. I keep one in my Bible.

The ten questions are as follows:

1. Have you been a testimony this week to the greatness of Jesus Christ with both your words and actions?
2. Have you been exposed to sexually alluring material or allowed your mind to entertain inappropriate thoughts about someone who is not your spouse this week?
3. Have you lacked any integrity in your financial dealings this week, or coveted something that does not belong to you?
4. Have you been honoring, understanding and generous in your important relationships this past week?
5. Have you damaged another person by your words, either behind their back or face-to-face?
6. Have you given in to an addictive behavior this week? Explain.
7. Have you continued to remain angry toward another?
8. Have you secretly wished for another's misfortune so that you might excel?
9. Did you finish your reading this week and hear from the Lord? What are you going to do about it?
10. Have you been completely honest with me?